GROWING DEEPER WITH GOD

LIFE MESSAGES OF
GREAT CHRISTIANS

Growing Deeper with God

~

OSWALD CHAMBERS

Compiled by
JUDITH COUCHMAN

SERVANT PUBLICATIONS
ANN ARBOR, MICHIGAN

Vine Books is an imprint of Servant Publications especially designed to serve
evangelical Christians.

Unless otherwise noted, Scripture verses have been taken from the King James Version of
the Bible. Scripture verses marked NIV have been taken from the HOLY BIBLE, NEW
INTERNATIONAL VERSION © 1973, 1978, 1984 by International Bible Society. Used
by permission of Zondervan Publishing House. All rights reserved. Verses marked RSV are
from the Revised Standard Version of the Bible, © 1946, 1952, 1971 by the Division of
Christian Education of the National Council of Churches of Christ in the USA. Used by
permission. Verses marked NRSV are from the New Revised Standard Version of the Bible,
© 1989 by the Division of Christian Education of the National Council of Churches of
Christ in the USA. Used by permission. All rights reserved.

Growing Deeper with God is compiled from the following works of Oswald Chambers and is
published by special arrangement with and permission of Discovery House Publishers, Box
3566, Grand Rapids, Michigan 49501.

Approved Unto God © 1946, 1948, 1997; *Biblical Ethics* © 1947; *Christian Disciplines* ©
1935, 1936, 1985, 1995; *Conformed to His Image* © 1950, 1996; *Facing Reality* © 1948,
1997; *God's Workmanship* © 1953; *If Thou Wilt Be Perfect* © 1941; *If Ye Shall Ask* ©
1937, 1958, 1985, 1989; *The Love of God* © 1938, 1973, 1985, 1988; *Moral Foundations
of Life* © 1966; *Not Knowing Whither* © 1934, 1989; *Our Brilliant Heritage* © 1929,
1930, 1931, 1975; *The Place of Help* © 1936, Dodd, Mead & Co., © 1989; *Shade of His
Hand* © 1936, 1991; *So Send I You* © 1930, 1993, © Oswald Chambers Publications
Assn., Ltd.

Published by Servant Publications
P.O. Box 8617
Ann Arbor, Michigan 48107

97 98 99 00   10 9 8 7 6 5 4 3 2 1

Printed in the United States of America
ISBN 1-56955-007-7

LIBRARY OF CONGRESS CATALOGING-IN-PUBLICATION DATA

Chambers, Oswald, 1874-1917
Growing deeper with God / Oswald Chambers ; compiled by Judith Couchman.
    p.   cm. — (Life messages of great Christians ; 5)
Includes bibliographical references.
ISBN 1-56955-007-7
1. Christian life.   I. Couchman, Judith, 1953-   . II. Title.   III. Series.
BV4501.2.C475   1997
248.4—dc21   97-7890
                                                                CIP

For Kathy Fisher,
who encouraged me to grow deeper.

Contents

Acknowledgments

~

I AM GRATEFUL FOR the editorial team at Servant Publications who contributed to this book's development: Bert Ghezzi, Liz Heaney, Heidi Hess, and Traci Mullins. Bob DeVries from Discovery House was also crucial to getting *Growing Deeper with God* to press by granting us the rights to reprint from Oswald Chambers' sermons. Working with these people, I am in the company of experts.

Shirley Honeywell cheerfully contributed her typing skills to this project, and Gwen Ellis contributed ideas and enthusiasm for the *Life Messages of Great Christians* series. Thanks so much; positive strokes motivate a writer.

Charette Barta, Opal Couchman, Win Couchman, Madalene Harris, Karen Hilt, Shirley Honeywell, Mae Lammers, and Nancy Lemons also deserve many thanks for their prayers as I worked on this book. When they pray, I am in the company of angels.

Introduction

∽

IN 1915, DURING THE GREAT WAR, a young Scotsman stood in his friend's kitchen, ready to say goodbye. "I am going out to Egypt to help the men in the armed forces," said the athletic-looking Oswald Chambers. "I have a Bible text: *I am now ready to be offered* (2 Timothy 4:6). I do not know what it means, but I am ready."[1]

This is how Oswald Chambers approached his spiritual life and calling. He didn't need to understand everything God wanted from him; it only mattered that he unwaveringly followed the Lord. This attitude of obedience led him from an artistic career into the ministry: first as an itinerant evangelist (1906-1910), then as a Bible college teacher (1911-1915), and finally as a spiritual shepherd to troops at war in Egypt (1915-1917). In all of his teaching, Oswald underscored the necessity of growing deeper with God.

Years before Oswald had written: *I feel I shall be buried for a time, hidden away in obscurity; then suddenly I shall flame out, do my work and be gone.*[2] His instincts proved true. While in Egypt the beloved teacher fell ill quickly and died at age forty-three.

From a physical viewpoint, God cut short His servant's life, but from a spiritual perspective, the obedient Scot still teaches us today. Nearly eighty years after his death, Oswald Chambers' teachings thrive through many still-in-print books, based on his wife Gertrude's shorthand notes of his sermons. In addition, his perennial devotional, *My Utmost for His Highest*, has sold millions of copies and ranks among the world's spiritual classics.

Such popularity would have surprised and embarrassed Oswald, who never intended for his works to be published. Typical of his self-effacing style, Oswald's gravestone simply states, "A believer in Jesus Christ," with an etched Bible opened to Luke 11:13: "If ye then, being evil, know how to give good gifts unto your children: how much more shall your heavenly Father give the Holy Spirit to them that ask him?"

Certainly, Oswald Chambers was God's good gift to His children, past, present, and future.

Judith Couchman
June, 1996

1. D. W. Lambert, *Oswald Chambers: An Unbribed Soul* (Fort Washington, PA: Christian Literature Crusade, 1983), 7.

2. Lambert, 27.

PART ONE

LEARNING GOD'S WAYS

O Lord, I am not weary of Thy pace,
nor weary of mine own patience.
I provoke Thee not with a prayer,
not with a wish,
not with a hope,
to more haste than consists with Thy purpose,
nor look that any other thing
should have entered into Thy purpose
but Thy glory.
To hear Thy steps coming towards me
is the same comfort
as to see Thy face present with me.
Whether Thou do the work of a thousand years
in a day,
or extend the work of a day
to a thousand years,
as long as Thou workest,
it is light and comfort.

John Donne, *Devotions Upon Emergent Occasions*

OSWALD CHAMBERS' INSIGHT
Thirsting for God is more important
than understanding all of His ways.

GETTING INTO GOD'S STRIDE

THOUGHT FOR TODAY

God wants us to cultivate His attitude about our calling in life.

WISDOM FROM SCRIPTURE

These things God has revealed to us through the Spirit; for the Spirit searches everything, even the depths of God.

For what human being knows what is truly human except the human spirit that is within? So also no one comprehends what is truly God's except the Spirit of God.

Now we have received not the spirit of the world, but the Spirit that is from God, so that we may understand the gifts bestowed on us by God.

And we speak of these things in words not taught by human wisdom but taught by the Spirit, interpreting spiritual things to those who are spiritual.

Those who are unspiritual do not receive the gifts of God's Spirit, for they are foolishness to them, and they are unable to understand them because they are spiritually discerned.

Those who are spiritual discern all things, and they are themselves subject to no one else's scrutiny.

"For who has known the mind of the Lord so as to instruct him?" But we have the mind of Christ.

1 CORINTHIANS 2:10-16, NRSV

INSIGHTS FROM OSWALD CHAMBERS

In learning to walk with God there is the difficulty of getting into His stride; when we have got into His stride, what manifests itself in the life is the characteristic of God. The idea in the Bible is not only that we might be saved, but that we might become sons and daughters of God, and that means having the attitude of God....

Moses was learned in all the wisdom of the Egyptians. He was a mighty man and a great statesman, and when he saw the oppression of his people he felt God had called him to deliver them, and in the righteous indignation of his own spirit he started to right their wrongs. God is never in a hurry. After the first big strike for God and for the right thing, God allowed Moses, the only man who could deliver his own people, to be driven into the desert to feed sheep—forty years of blank discouragement....

We may have a vision of God, a very clear understanding of what God wants—wrongs to be righted, the salvation of sinners, and the sanctification of believers; we are certain we see the way out, and we start to do the thing. Then comes something equivalent to the forty years in the wilderness: discouragement, disaster, upset, as if God has ignored the whole thing. When we are thoroughly flattened out, God comes back and revives the call, and we ... say, "Oh, who am I, that I should go?"

We have to learn the first great stride of God—"I AM WHO I AM ... has sent ... you" (Exodus 3:14). We have to learn that our individual effort for God is an impertinence; our individuality must be rendered incandescent by a personal relationship to God, and that is not learned easily. The individual man is lost in a personal union with God, and what is manifested is the stride and power of God....

Saul of Tarsus was "knocked out," and it took him three days to get his breath before he could begin to get into the stride of God. Who was Saul of Tarsus? A Pharisee of Pharisees, a man of superb integrity and conscientiousness. If there ever was a conscientious objector, it was Saul. [He admitted,] "Indeed, I myself thought I must do many things contrary to the name of Jesus of Nazareth" (Acts 26:9). He was conscientious when he hounded the followers of Jesus Christ to death.

Then came disaster; all his world was flung to pieces. God arrested him. [The Bible says,] "He was three days without sight, and neither ate nor drank," but out of the inscrutable disaster and upset, God brought him into a personal experience of Himself. [Paul later explained,] "But when it pleased God, who separated me from my mother's womb and called me through His grace, to reveal His Son in me, that I might preach Him among the Gentiles, I did not immediately confer with flesh and blood" (Galatians 1:15-16). For three years Saul went round about Sinai while the Holy Spirit blazed into him the things that became his Epistles....

...God's Spirit alters the atmosphere of our ways of looking at things, and things begin to be possible which never were possible before. If you are going through a period of discouragement there is a big personal enlargement ahead. We have the stride of divine healing, of sanctification, of the second coming; all these are right, but the stride of God is never anything less than union with Himself.

—The Place of Help

Questions to Consider
1. How could you begin to get into God's stride?
2. How might adapting God's mindset affect your approach to a spiritual calling?

A Prayerful Response
Lord, prompt me to get into Your stride and attitude about my spiritual calling. Amen.

At God's Discretion

Thought for Today

As we obey Him, God reveals more of His mysterious ways to us.

Wisdom from Scripture

For the gifts and the calling of God are irrevocable.

Just as you were once disobedient to God but have now received mercy because of their disobedience, so they have now been disobedient in order that, by the mercy shown to you, they too may now receive mercy.

For God has imprisoned all in disobedience so that he may be merciful to all.

O the depth of the riches and wisdom and knowledge of God! How unsearchable are his judgments and how inscrutable his ways!

"For who has known the mind of the Lord? Or who has been his counselor?"

"Or who has given a gift to him, to receive a gift in return?"

For from him and through him and to him are all things. To him be the glory forever. Amen.

ROMANS 11:29-36, NRSV

Insights from Oswald Chambers

"Oh, the depth of the riches both of the wisdom and knowledge of God! How unsearchable are His judgments, and His ways past finding out" (Romans 11:33).

The purpose of mystery is not to tantalize us and make us feel that we cannot comprehend; it is a generous purpose, and meant to assure us that slowly and surely as we can bear it, the full revelation of God will be made clear....

It is only by way of obedience that we understand the teaching of God. Bring it straight down to the commonplace things: Have I done the duty that lies nearest? Have I obeyed God there? If not, I shall never fathom the mysteries of God, however much I may try. When once I obey there, I receive a revelation of the meaning of God's teaching for me. How many of us have obeyed the bit of God's truth we already know?

Experience is a gateway to understanding, not an end in itself. We can be bound in other ways than by sin; we can be bound by the limits of the very experiences meant to lead us into the secrets of God. The faith of many really spiritual Christians is eclipsed today ... [because] they tried to remain true and consistent to the narrow confines of their experience instead of getting out into the light of God. God wants to get us into the place where He holds us absolutely and experiences never bother us.

Oh the relief of it! The burden gone, the effort gone, no conscious experience left, because Jesus Christ is all and in all.

God has hidden the glory of His teaching in the experience of temptation. "My brethren, count it all joy when you fall into various trials," said the Apostle James (James 1:2).... We learn to thank God for the trial of our faith because it works patience. Precious in the sight of God is a faith that has been tried. Tried faith is spendable; it is so much wealth stored up in heaven and the more we go through the trial of our faith, the wealthier we become in the heavenly regions....

...God conceals His treasures in embarrassments, that is, in things that involve us in difficulty. [He said,] "I will give you the treasures of darkness" (Isaiah 45:3). We should never have suspected that treasures were hidden there, and in order to get them we have to go through things that involve us in perplexity. There is nothing more wearying to the eye than perpetual sunshine, and the same is true spiritually. The valley of the shadow gives us time to reflect, and we learn to praise God for the valley because our soul was restored in its communion with God.

God gives us a new revelation of His kindness in the valley of the shadow (Psalms 23:4). What are the days and experiences that have furthered us most? The days of green pastures, of absolute ease? No, they have their value; but the days that have furthered us most in character are the days of stress and cloud … the days when we could not see our way but had to stand still and wait; and, as we waited, the comforting and sustaining and restoring of God came in a way we never before imagined possible.

God wants us to realize His sovereignty. We are apt to tie God up in His own laws and allow Him no free will. We say we know what God will do, and suddenly He upsets all our calculations by working in unprecedented ways. Just when we expected He would do a certain thing, He did the opposite. There are unexpected issues in life—unexpected joys when we looked for sorrow, and sorrow when we expected joy—until we learn to say "my expectation is from Him" (Psalm 62:5).

Again, God disciplines us by disappointment. Life may have been like a torrent, then suddenly down comes a barrier of disappointment, until slowly we learn that the disappointment was His appointment. God hides His treasures in darkness, and many a radiant star that was not seen before comes out. In some lives you can see the treasure; there is a sweetness and beauty about them, "the incorruptible ornament of a gentle and quiet spirit" (1 Peter 3:4), and you wonder where the winsome power of God came from. It came from the dark places where God revealed His sovereign will in unexpected issues....

"It is the glory of God to conceal a matter" (Proverbs 25:2, NIV). God will not have us come with an impatient curiosity. Moral or intellectual or spiritual insanity results if we push barriers which God has placed before our spiritual progress is fit for the revelation....

God grant we may accept His clouds and mysteries, and be led into His inner secrets by obedient trust.

—*The Place of Help*

Questions to Consider

1. What might God be teaching you through temptation or disappointment?
2. What could be the specific purpose of God's barriers around you right now?

A Prayerful Response

Lord, I accept my setbacks in life as divine appointments from You. Amen.

WHY ARE WE NOT TOLD PLAINLY?

THOUGHT FOR TODAY

God unveils truths to us when we are spiritually ready for them.

WISDOM FROM SCRIPTURE

[Jesus said,] "Nevertheless I tell you the truth: it is to your advantage that I go away, for if I do not go away, the Advocate will not come to you; but if I go, I will send him to you.

"And when he comes, he will prove the world wrong about sin and righteousness and judgment: about sin, because they do not believe in me; about righteousness, because I am going to the Father and you will see me no longer; about judgment, because the ruler of this world has been condemned.

"I still have many things to say to you, but you cannot bear them now.

"When the Spirit of truth comes, he will guide you into all the truth; for he will not speak on his own, but will speak whatever he hears, and he will declare to you the things that are to come.

"He will glorify me, because he will take what is mine and declare it to you.

"All that the Father has is mine. For this reason I said that he will take what is mine and declare it to you.

"A little while, and you will no longer see me, and again a little while, and you will see me."

JOHN 16:7-16, NRSV

INSIGHTS FROM OSWALD CHAMBERS

"I still have many things to say to you, but you cannot bear them now" (John 16:12, NRSV).

Our Lord does not hide things from us, but they are unbearable until we are in a fit condition of spiritual life to receive them; then the word our Lord has spoken becomes so plain that we are amazed we did not understand it before. We could not understand it before because we were not in the place either in disposition or in will where it could be borne. There must be communion with the resurrection life of Jesus before a particular word can be borne of us....

Obtuseness is valuable sometimes. It is of God's infinite mercy that we do not understand what He says until we are in a fit condition. If God came down with His light and power, we should be witless. But our Lord never enthralls us. Satan tempted Jesus to use the power of enthrallment, and false methods of service are built up on that line. When we first know the Lord ... our prayers are really dictation to God. God will take us out of the obtuse stage as soon as we let the resurrection life of Jesus have its way with us.

Do we know anything about the impartation of the risen life of Jesus Christ? The evidence that we do is that His words are becoming interpretable to us. God cannot reveal anything to us if we have not His Spirit. If we have made up our minds about a doctrine, we cannot get any more light from God about it.... An obstinate outlook will effectually hinder God's revealing anything to us. It is not sin, but unenlightenment caused by the absence of the resurrection life of Jesus....

We need to rely much deeper down consciously on the resurrection life of Jesus, to get into the habit of steadily referring everything back to Him. Instead of that, we make our common sense decisions and say we hope God will bless them. He cannot. They are not in His domain.... As God's children we are to walk in the light of the Lord. When we do things from a sense of duty, we can back it up by argument; but when we do things out of obedience to the Lord there is no logical argument possible. That is why a saint can easily be ridiculed....

Is Jesus Christ risen in us? Is He getting His way? When we look back on the choice of our life work, of our friends, of what we call our duty, is He the dominating one? We can soon know whether He is.... Many a Christian worker has ... gone into work from a sense of duty woven out of a need, or of a call arising from his own particular discernment. There is no sin in it, and no punishment attached, but when that one realizes he has hindered his understanding of what Jesus says and produced for himself perplexities and sorrows, it is with shame and contrition he has to come back like a little child and ask the Lord to teach him all over again.

When we do a thing from a sense of duty, the childlike attitude is gone. The power of the resurrection life of Jesus is not there. We have put up a standard in competition with our Lord and have gotten out of contact with Him....

"The time is coming when I ... will tell you plainly about the Father" (John 16:25)....

When is that day? When the resurrection life of the Lord Jesus is the portion of our life. In that day we shall be one with the Father ... because the Holy Spirit has brought us there. No one can receive the Holy Spirit unless he is convinced of his own poverty. When we receive the Holy Spirit, He imparts the risen life of Jesus and there is no distance between the Father and His child.

Have we come to this unquestioning place where there is no more perplexity of heart in regard to God? Any number of things may be dark and unexplained, but they do not come in between the heart and God.... "Let not your heart be troubled" (John 14:1) [can become] the real state of your life. Until the resurrection life of Jesus Christ is manifested, we want to ask questions; whenever we take a new step in God's providence we want to ask this and that. When the point of entire reliance on the resurrection of Jesus is reached, and we are brought into perfect contact with the purpose of God, we find our questions have gone.

Are we living that life now? If not, why shouldn't we?

What makes us say, "I wish God would tell me plainly?" Never look for an explanation from without or in your own mind; look for it in your disposition. The reason anything is a mystery and is coming between yourself and God is in the disposition, not the intellect. When once the disposition is willingly submitted to the life of Jesus, the understanding becomes perfectly clear.

—The Place of Help

QUESTIONS TO CONSIDER
1. What spiritual truths do you want God to reveal to you?
2. How, specifically, can you prepare to receive those truths?

A PRAYERFUL RESPONSE
Lord, teach me to rely more on You so I can better understand Your ways. Amen.

WITH GOD AT THE FRONT

THOUGHT FOR TODAY

God fulfills His purposes through people who recognize their spiritual poverty.

WISDOM FROM SCRIPTURE

For since, in the wisdom of God, the world did not know God through wisdom, God decided, through the foolishness of our proclamation, to save those who believe.

For Jews demand signs and Greeks desire wisdom, but we proclaim Christ crucified, a stumbling block to Jews and foolishness to Gentiles, but to those who are the called, both Jews and Greeks, Christ the power of God and the wisdom of God.

For God's foolishness is wiser than human wisdom, and God's weakness is stronger than human strength.

Consider your own call, brothers and sisters: not many of you were wise by human standards, not many were powerful, not many were of noble birth.

But God chose what is foolish in the world to shame the wise; God chose what is weak in the world to shame the strong; God chose what is low and despised in the world, things that are not, to reduce to nothing things that are, so that no one might boast in the presence of God.

He is the source of your life in Christ Jesus, who became for us wisdom from God, and righteousness and sanctification and redemption, in order that, as it is written, "Let the one who boasts, boast in the Lord."

1 CORINTHIANS 1:21-31, NRSV

The bravery of God in trusting us! It is a tremendously risky thing to do; it looks as if all the odds [are] against Him. The majority of us don't bother much about Him, and yet He deliberately stakes all He has on us. He stands by and lets the world, the flesh, and the devil do their worst, confident we will come out all right....

We say, "It seems out of all proportion that God should choose me. I am of no value." The reason He chooses us is that we are not of any value. It is folly to think that because a man has natural ability, he must make a good Christian. People with the best natural equipment may make the worst disciples because they will "boss" themselves. It is not a question of our equipment, but of our poverty; not what we bring with us, but what He puts in us; not our natural virtues, our strength of character, our knowledge, our experience. All that is of no avail...; the only thing that avails is that we are taken up into the big compelling of God and being made His comrade (1 Corinthians 1:26-28). His comradeship is made out of men who know their poverty. God can do nothing with men who think they will be of use to Him.... We are not out for "our cause" as Christians, we are out for the cause of God, which can never be our cause. It is not that God is on our side; we must see that we are on God's side, which is a different matter. We do not know what God is after, but we have to maintain our relationship with Him, whatever happens....

God called Jesus Christ to unmitigated distaste; Jesus Christ called His disciples to come and see Him put to death; He led every one of those disciples to the place where their hearts broke. The whole thing was an absolute failure from every standpoint but God's, and yet the thing that was the biggest failure from man's standpoint was the ultimate triumph from God's, because God's purpose was not man's.

In our own lives there comes the baffling call of God. "Let us go over to the other side [of the lake]," Jesus said to His disciples (Mark 4:35). They obeyed, but as soon as they got into the boat there arose a great storm of wind and there was a squall that nearly drowned them. The call of God cannot be stated explicitly; it is implicit. The call of God is like the call of the sea: no one hears it but the person who has the nature of the sea in him.

You cannot state definitely what the call of God is to; it is to be in comradeship with God for His own purposes, and the test of faith is to believe God knows what He is after. The fact that history fulfills prophecy is a small matter compared to our maintenance of a right relationship to God, who is working out His purposes. The things that happen do not happen by chance at all; they happen entirely in the decrees of God.

To be "with God at the front" means the continual maintenance of our relationship to Him. If I maintain communion with God and recognize that He is taking me up into His purposes, I will no longer try to find out what those purposes are.... If God has been brave enough to trust me, surely it is up to me not to let Him down, but to "hang in."

You say, "God has been very unwise to choose me because there is nothing in me." As long as there is something in you He cannot choose you, because you have your own ends to serve. But if you let Him bring you to the end of your self-sufficiency, then He can choose you to go with Him to Jerusalem, and that means the fulfillment of His purposes, which He does not discuss with you at all. We go on with Him, and in the final wind-up, the glory of God will be manifested before our eyes.... We may take what ways we like, but behind them come the big compellings of God. The Christian

28

is one who trusts the wisdom of God, not his own wits. astute mind behind the saint's life is the mind of God, not own mind.

—*The Place of Help*

Questions to Consider

1. What does "spiritual poverty" mean to you?
2. How might recognizing your spiritual poverty affect how you live?

A Prayerful Response

Lord, I set aside my purposes for Yours. Amen.

GOD'S ORDER OF THINGS

THOUGHT FOR TODAY

Amidst the world's injustices, we can hold on to God's will for us.

WISDOM FROM SCRIPTURE

If you see the poor oppressed in a district, and justice and rights denied, do not be surprised at such things; for one official is eyed by a higher one, and over them both are others higher still.

The increase from the land is taken by all; the king himself profits from the fields.

Whoever loves money never has money enough; whoever loves wealth is never satisfied with his income. This too is meaningless.

As goods increase, so do those who consume them. And what benefit are they to the owner except to feast his eyes on them?

The sleep of a laborer is sweet, whether he eats little or much, but the abundance of a rich man permits him no sleep.

I have seen a grievous evil under the sun: wealth hoarded to the harm of its owner, or wealth lost through some misfortune, so that when he has a son there is nothing left for him.

Naked a man comes from his mother's womb, and as he comes, so he departs. He takes nothing from his labor that he can carry in his hand....

Then I realized that it is good and proper for a man to eat and drink, and to find satisfaction in his toilsome labor under the sun during the few days of life God has given him—for this is his lot.

Moreover, when God gives any man wealth and possessions, and enables him to enjoy them, to accept his lot and be happy in his work—this is a gift of God.

He seldom reflects on the days of his life, because God keeps him occupied with gladness of heart.

ECCLESIASTES 5:8-15, 18-20, NIV

INSIGHTS FROM OSWALD CHAMBERS

All through the Bible the difference between God's order and God's permissive will is brought out. God's permissive will is the things that are now, whether they are right or wrong. If you are looking for justice, you will come to the conclusion that God is the devil, and if the providential order of things today were God's order, then that conclusion would be right. But if the order of things today is God's permissive will, that is quite another matter.

We have to get hold of God's order in the midst of His permissive will. God may bring many "sons" to glory. A son is more than a saved soul; a son is one who has been through the fight and stood the test and come out sterlingly worthy. The Bible's attitude to things is absolutely robust—there is not the tiniest whine about it. There is no possibility of lying like limp jellyfish on God's providence; it is never allowed for a second. There is always a sting and a kick all through the Bible.

Solomon says when you see the providential order of tyranny, don't be amazed at it. According to the Bible the explanation is that the basis of things is tragic; things have gone wrong and they can only be put right and brought into God's order by the individual relationship of men and women [to Him]. We find tyranny everywhere [and we] take it in a personal way: we all think we are the creatures of injustice. There never was a man who was not!...

If I expect to see everything in the universe as good and right and I find it is not, I get faint-hearted. Solomon won't have us go off on the limb of the abstract and say these things ought not to be; they are! Injustice and lust...and murder and crime and bestiality and grabbing are as thick as desert sand, and it is cowardly for a person to say because these things are as they are, therefore he must drift [spiritually].

We say we had to take a particular course because the prevailing trend of God's providence was that way. It is a remarkable thing that two boats can sail in opposite directions in the same wind; they can go according to the steering skill of the pilot and not according to the prevailing wind. In the same way a man can trim his sails and grasp hold of God's order however much it costs him.

The earth is cursed because of man's apostasy, and when that apostasy ceases in actual history, the ground will no longer bring forth the curse. The final redemption includes "new heavens and a new earth" (Isaiah 65:17). Instead of the thorn shall come up the cypress tree, and "the wolf also shall lie down with the lamb" (Isaiah 11:6). Instead of the savage ferocity of the beasts, there will be the strength without the savageness—an inconceivable order of things just now....

The curious thing about civilization is that it tends to take men away from the soil and makes them develop an artificial existence away from the elemental. Civilization has become an elaborate way of doing without God, and when civilized life [receives] a smashing blow by tyranny, most of us have not a leg to stand on.

Solomon reminds us that king and peasant alike can only gain their profit by proper tillage of the soil (Ecclesiastes 5:9). The laws given in the Bible include a scheme for the treatment of the earth and they insist on proper rest being given to the land, and make it clear that that alone will bring profit.... Leviticus 25 is the great classic on the rights of the earth.

"He who loves silver will not be satisfied with silver; nor he who loves abundance, with increase. This also is vanity. When goods increase, they increase who eat them; so what profit have the owners except to see them with their eyes?" (Ecclesiastes 5:10-11).

To make treasure is different from making profit. Treasure is the thing that is esteemed for itself, not for what it brings. The Bible tirades against possession for possession's sake. "Lay up for yourselves treasures in heaven ... for where your treasure is, there will your heart be also" (Matthew 6:20-21, RSV).

If your treasure is in God or in land or the possessions of earth, that is where your heart will be, and when wars and rumors of wars arise, your heart will fail you for fear. If a man has his treasure vested in bonds and a war strikes, how can he keep his mind at rest? Panic and devastation and ruin are the result—profitless in every degree.

The manipulation of civilized life has not resulted in the development of the tillage of the land, but in the building up of treasure, and it is not only the miser who grabs. The sense of possession is a snare to a true spiritual life. Paul uses the life of a soldier to illustrate a saint's life (see 2 Timothy 2:3-4). No sense of property or possession can go along with an abiding detachment [that God asks of us].

In civilized life it is the building up of possessions that is the snare: "This is my house, my land. There are my books, and my things." Imagine when they are touched! I am consumed with distress. Over and over again Jesus Christ drives this point home: Remember, don't have your heart in your possessions; let them come and go.

Solomon warns about the same thing: Whatever possessions you have will consume the nobility of your life in an appalling way. In the case of Job, Satan asked permission to play havoc with his possessions and God gave him permission, and every possession Job had, even to his bodily health, went. But Job proved that a man would remain true to his love of God though all his possessions went to rack and ruin.

—Shade of His Hand

QUESTIONS TO CONSIDER

1. What injustice affects your life today? How do you feel about it?
2. How can you discern God's order, despite this injustice?

A PRAYERFUL RESPONSE

Lord, in the midst of life's injustices, show me Your order and purpose. Amen.

GOD IS GOOD

THOUGHT FOR TODAY

God is good, and faithful to fulfill His promises.

WISDOM FROM SCRIPTURE

After this, the word of the LORD came to Abram in a vision: "Do not be afraid, Abram. I am your shield, your very great reward."

But Abram said, "O Sovereign LORD, what can you give me since I remain childless and the one who will inherit my estate is Eliezer of Damascus?"

And Abram said, "You have given me no children; so a servant in my household will be my heir."

Then the word of the LORD came to him: "This man will not be your heir, but a son coming from your own body will be your heir."

He took him outside and said, "Look up at the heavens and count the stars—if indeed you can count them." Then he said to him, "So shall your offspring be."

Abram believed the LORD, and he credited it to him as righteousness.

Now the LORD was gracious to Sarah as he had said, and the LORD did for Sarah what he had promised.

Sarah became pregnant and bore a son to Abraham in his old age, at the very time God had promised him.

Abraham gave the name Isaac to the son Sarah bore him.

When his son Isaac was eight days old, Abraham circumcised him, as God commanded him.

Abraham was a hundred years old when his son Isaac was born to him.

Sarah said, "God has brought me laughter, and everyone who hears about this will laugh with me."

GENESIS 15:1-6; 21:1-6, NRSV

INSIGHTS FROM OSWALD CHAMBERS

One of the greatest demands on the human spirit is to believe that God is good when His providence seems to prohibit the fulfillment of what He has promised. The one character in the Bible who sustains this strain grandly is Abraham. Paul, in summing up the life of Abraham, pointed to this as his greatest quality: "Abraham believed God" (Romans 4:3).

No one can fulfill a promise but the one who makes it. These words contain the whole autobiography of the godly ups and downs of the life of faith. During the years when everything seemed to contradict the fulfillment of the promise, Abraham continually forgot this fundamental fact and tried to help God keep His promise. God alone can fulfill His promises, and we have to come to the place of perfect reliance upon God to do just that (see 1 Thessalonians 5:23-24).

Just as the Lord visited Sarah "as He had said," He visits the believer with the word of promise and visits him again with the word of fulfillment. Abraham endured for twenty-five years without any sign of fulfillment. The majority of us know nothing about waiting; we don't wait, we endure. Faithful waiting means that we go on in the perfect certainty of God's goodness—no dumps or fears.

[In Abraham's case,] the presentation of God's performance was in the birth of an ordinary child, extraordinary only to the eye of faith. We come not with faith in His goodness but with a conception of our own, and we look for God to come to us in that way. God cannot come to us in our way; He can only come in His own way—in ways man would never dream of looking for Him. In the Incarnation the eternal God was so majestically small that the world never saw Him. And this is still true today. We cry out, "Oh God, I wish You would come to me," when He is there all the time. Then suddenly we see Him and say, "Surely the Lord is in this place, and I knew it not" (Genesis 28:16).

We expect desolation and anguish; instead there is laughter and hilarity when we see God. This astonishment at the performance of God is brought out over and over again until we learn to be humiliated at our despicable disbelief....

There is no relation between the promise of God for the life He forms in us by regeneration and our personal, private ambitions; those ambitions are completely transfigured. We must heed the promise of God and see that we do not try to make God's gift fulfill our own ends.

Suppose that God sees fit to put us into desolation when He begins the forming of His Son in us. What ought it to matter? All He is after in you and me is the forming of His Son in us. When He drives the sword through the natural, we begin to whine and say, "Oh, I can't go through that." But we must go through it. If we refuse to make our natural life obedient to the Son of God in us, the Son of God will be put to death in us. We have to "put on the new man" (Ephesians 4:24) in our human nature to fit the life of the Son of God in us, and see that in ... our bodily lives we conduct our life for Him.

Sarah's hilarity is the joy of God sounding through the upset equilibrium of a mind that scarcely expected the promise to be fulfilled (see Genesis 21:6). The son of Sarah is himself a type of the Son of Mary, and in each case the promise is limited through a particular woman and through an apparently impossible, yet actual, birth.... God's ways turn man's thinking upside down.

Amazement comes when God's promise is fulfilled (see Genesis 21:7). What is known as the dark side of Christian experience is not really Christian experience at all; it is God putting the rot of sacramental death through the natural virtues in order to produce something in keeping with His Son.... All our whining and misery ought to be the laughter of Sarah: "Now I see what God wants!" Instead, we moan in corners and gloom before God and say, "I am afraid I am not sanctified."

If we fight against the desolation, we will kill the life of God in us. Yield to it, and God's fulfillment will amaze us. It is in the periods of desolation that the sickly pietists talk about, "What I am suffering!" They are in the initial stages and have not begun to realize God's purpose. God is working out the manifestation of the fulfillment of His promise, and when it is fulfilled there is never any thought of self or of self-consideration anywhere.

—Not Knowing Whither

QUESTIONS TO CONSIDER
1. What has been your response to God's unfulfilled promises to you?
2. What would it mean to yield to God's timing for fulfilling these promises?

A PRAYERFUL RESPONSE
Lord, I trust that at the right time, You will fulfill Your promises to me. Amen.

GOD TAKES HIS TIME

THOUGHT FOR TODAY

When we try to speed up God's plan, we can delay or destroy it.

WISDOM FROM SCRIPTURE

Now Sarai, Abram's wife, had borne him no children. But she had an Egyptian maidservant named Hagar; so she said to Abram, "The LORD has kept me from having children. Go, sleep with my maidservant; perhaps I can build a family through her." Abram agreed to what Sarai said.

So after Abram had been living in Canaan ten years, Sarai his wife took her Egyptian maidservant Hagar and gave her to her husband to be his wife.

He slept with Hagar, and she conceived. When she knew she was pregnant, she began to despise her mistress.

Then Sarai said to Abram, "You are responsible for the wrong I am suffering. I put my servant in your arms, and now that she knows she is pregnant, she despises me. May the LORD judge between you and me."

"Your servant is in your hands," Abram said. "Do with her whatever you think best." Then Sarai mistreated Hagar; so she fled from her.

The angel of the LORD found Hagar near a spring in the desert; it was the spring that is beside the road to Shur.

And he said, "Hagar, servant of Sarai, where have you come from, and where are you going?"

"I'm running away from my mistress Sarai," she answered.

Then the angel of the LORD told her, "Go back to your mistress and submit to her."

The angel added, "I will so increase your descendants that they will be too numerous to count."

The angel of the LORD also said to her: "You are now with child and you will have a son. You shall name him Ishmael, for the LORD has heard of your misery. He will be a wild donkey of a man; his hand will be against everyone and everyone's hand against him, and he will live in hostility toward all his brothers."

She gave this name to the LORD who spoke to her: "You are the God who sees me," for she said, "I have now seen the One who sees me."

So Hagar bore Abram a son, and Abram gave the name Ishmael to the son she had borne.

GENESIS 16:1-13, 15, NRSV

INSIGHTS FROM OSWALD CHAMBERS

The word of the Lord came to Abraham in a vision. God's method always seems to be vision first and then reality, but in between the vision and reality there is often a deep valley of humiliation....

Whenever God gives a vision to a saint, He puts the saint in the shadow of His hand and the saint's duty is to be still and listen.... [There is] danger in listening to "good advice" in the dark instead of waiting for God to send the light.

When God gives a vision and darkness follows, wait. God will bring you into accordance with the vision He has given you, if you will await His timing. Otherwise, you try to do away with the supernatural in God's undertakings. Never try to help God fulfill His word. There are some things we cannot do, and that is one of them.

We must never try to anticipate the actual fulfillment of a vision. Often we transact some business spiritually with God on our mount of transfiguration and by faith see clearly a vision of His purpose; then immediately afterward there is nothing but blank darkness. We trust in the Lord, but we walk in darkness.

At that point we are tempted to work up enthusiasm. Instead, we are to wait on God. If darkness turns to spiritual doldrums, we are to blame. When God puts the dark of "nothing" into our experience, it is the most positive "something" He can give to us. If we do anything at that point it is sure to be wrong. We need to stay in the center of nothing and say "thank You" for it. When God gives us nothing it means we are inside Him, and by determining to do something we put ourselves outside Him. This is a great lesson that few of us seem to learn.

Abraham would not stay in the land when the famine came because there was nothing; He would not trust God for a child because there was no one. God kept giving Abraham nothing (except Himself), and by determining to do "something" Abraham jumped outside God and found that he was putting himself in the relationship of the Everlasting No.

There are things God tells us to do without any light or illumination other than the word of His command. All of God's commands are enablings. We must not be weak in His strength.

Abraham had anticipated the purpose of God and had to pass through a long time of discipline. The act of Abraham and Sarah [creating a child with Hagar] produced a complexity in God's plan that echoed down through the ages. In the same way, Moses had to wait forty years after his presumptuous attempt to reach his destination.

Adam and Eve did the same thing when they tried to take the "shortcut" (which is the meaning of temptation) and anticipated their destination to be *actually* what they were *potentially* and thereby went wrong. Temptation does not spring from selfish lust, but from a passionate desire to reach God's destination.

Abraham emerged out of this stage of discipline with one determination: to let God have His way. There is no indication that he is relying on the flesh any longer; his reliance is on God alone. All self-sufficiency has been destroyed. There is not one common-sense ray left as to how God is going to fulfill His word.

God never hastens and He never tarries. He works His plans out in His own way, and we either lie like clogs in His hands or we assist Him by being as clay in the hands of the Potter.

Now Abraham sees the real God, not a vision. Such knowledge of the real God is reached when our confidence is placed in God and not in His blessings. Abraham's faith became a tried faith built on a real God.

—Not Knowing Whither

QUESTIONS TO CONSIDER

1. Have you ever tried to assist God in fulfilling His promises? If so, what happened?
2. How can you become clay in the Potter's hands as He works out His promises to you?

A PRAYERFUL RESPONSE

Lord, I will be clay in the Potter's hands, submitting to Your way of fulfilling Your promises. Amen.

THE PATH OF GOD

THOUGHT FOR TODAY

God's path leads to a Person, not just a plan.

WISDOM FROM SCRIPTURE

Isaac said to his father Abraham, "Father!" And he said, "Here I am, my son." He said, "The fire and the wood are here, but where is the lamb for a burnt offering?"

Abraham said, "God himself will provide the lamb for a burnt offering, my son." So the two of them walked on together.

When they came to the place that God had shown him, Abraham built an altar there and laid the wood in order. He bound his son Isaac, and laid him on the altar, on top of the wood.

Then Abraham reached out his hand and took the knife to kill his son.

But the angel of the LORD called to him from heaven, and said, "Abraham, Abraham!" And he said, "Here I am."

He said, "Do not lay your hand on the boy or do anything to him; for now I know that you fear God, since you have not withheld your son, your only son, from me."

And Abraham looked up and saw a ram, caught in a thicket by its horns. Abraham went and took the ram and offered it up as a burnt offering instead of his son.

So Abraham called that place "The LORD will provide"; as it is said to this day, "On the mount of the LORD it shall be provided."

GENESIS 22:7-14, NRSV

The life of Abraham provides a pattern for...the soul's path to God. The turning points in his spiral ascent of faith are obedience to the effectual call of God and the culmination of unreserved resignation to God.

Abraham and Isaac were spiritually silent: the son was silent before the father, and the father was silent before God, and thus God elevated them both above unspiritual human nature. That is, both father and son went one step beyond the limit of the possible because they were on the path of God. To talk easily about spiritual experiences is an indication that we have only a devout nodding acquaintance with the experiences of others and are devoid of all such experiences ourselves.

... If we have never heard the call of God, all we see is the accountability that we can state to ourselves. Practical work is nearly always a determination to think for ourselves, to take the pressure of forethought on ourselves: "I see the need; therefore I must do something." That is not the effectual call of God, but the call of our sympathy with conditions as we see them. When God's call comes, we learn to do actively what He tells us and take no thought for the morrow. Take a step of faith in God, and your rational friends will say: "Very beautiful, but suppose we all did it!" You are not living a life of accountable rationality, but a life of agreement with God's effectual call, and therefore have no reply to make.

In Hebrews 11:17-19 we get further insight into Abraham's spirituality: "By faith Abraham, when he was tested, offered up Isaac ... of whom it was said, 'In Isaac your seed shall be called,' concluding that God was able to raise him up, even from the dead." It was not Abraham's common sense but his spiritual illumination that made him know this. However, beware of turning a common-sense somersault and saying that Abraham knew all about it, and therefore it was not a sacrifice at all. Abraham did not know all about it; he believed that somehow God would give Isaac back to him.

But how? He had no notion. He surrendered himself entirely to the supernatural God.

Abraham was prepared to do anything for God. Mark the difference between that and doing anything to prove your love to God. Abraham was there to obey God, no matter what that entailed. Abraham was not devoted to his own convictions.... Faith means giving up your own convictions and traditional beliefs.

He did not make declarations, as Peter did: "I will do anything; I will go to death for you" (Matthew 26:35). Instead, he remained true to God Himself, and God purified his faith. If we will remain true to God, He will lead us straight through the ordeal into the inner chamber of a better knowledge of Himself.

The sacrifice of death is not the final thing God wants. What God wants is the sacrifice through death which enables a man to do what Jesus did—that is, sacrifice his life (see Romans 12:1). Many of us think God wants us to give up things; we make Christianity the great apotheosis of giving up! God purified Abraham from this blunder, and the same discipline goes on in our lives.

God nowhere tells us to give up things just for the sake of giving them up. He tells us to give them up for the sake of the only thing worth having—life with Himself. It is a question of loosening the bands that hinder us, and as soon as they are loosened by identification with the death of Jesus, we enter into a relationship with God whereby we sacrifice our life to God....

Abraham did not receive an overt command to sacrifice the

ram; he recognized in the ram a divine suggestion. When people are intimate with one another, they can communicate by the power of suggestion, and when we come into true fellowship with God, we recognize His suggestions.

—Not Knowing Whither

QUESTIONS TO CONSIDER
1. How can you increase your devotion to God's voice?
2. What might His voice be suggesting to you today?

A PRAYERFUL RESPONSE
Lord, please help me to recognize Your voice, Your suggestions, Your path. Amen.

DAY 9

Obedience and Reward

Thought for Today

God asks for our willing obedience; then He bestows the joyous reward.

Wisdom from Scripture

The angel of the LORD called to Abraham a second time from heaven, and said, "By myself I have sworn, says the LORD: Because you have done this, and have not withheld your son, your only son, I will indeed bless you, and I will make your offspring as numerous as the stars of heaven and as the sand that is on the seashore.

"And your offspring shall possess the gate of their enemies, and by your offspring shall all the nations of the earth gain blessing for themselves, because you have obeyed my voice."

So Abraham returned to his young men, and they arose and went together to Beer-sheba; and Abraham lived at Beer-sheba.

GENESIS 22:15-19, NRSV

Insights from Oswald Chambers

The spirit of obedience gives more joy to God than anything else on earth.

Obedience is impossible to us naturally; even when we do obey, we do it with a pout in our moral underlip and with the determination to scale some moral ladder. In the spiritual domain there is no pout on our face because the nature of God has come into us. When the love of God is shed abroad in our hearts by the Holy Ghost (see Romans 5:5), we are possessed by the nature of God—and the great characteristic of our Lord's life was obedience.

By our obedience, we show that we love Him. The best measure of a spiritual life is not its ecstasies, but its obedience. "To obey is better than sacrifice" (1 Samuel 15:22).

When God first called to Abraham, there was still a dim gulf between them; God had to call and Abraham [had] to answer (see Genesis 22:1). Now that gulf is bridged. Abraham is so near to God that he does not need to reply; he is in the place of unimpeded listening. It makes us ask, "Is there any impediment between my ears and God's voice?"

The call of God is in accordance with the nature of God, not in accordance with my idea of God. At first Abraham did not interpret the call this way because he did not understand the nature of God; he interpreted it according to the Chaldean tradition and took it to mean he was to kill his son. The supreme crisis in Abraham's faith had now been reached; all his imperfect conceptions of God had been left behind and he now understood God as He is…. [Abraham] simply believed God.

Abraham had come to the place where he was in touch with the very nature of God; he understood the reality of God, and God unveiled Himself in a burst of enthusiasm. There is no possibility of questioning when God speaks to His own nature in us; prompt obedience is the only possible response. When Jesus says, "Come unto Me," we simply come; When He says, "Trust in God in this matter," we do not try to trust; we do trust. An alteration has taken place in our disposition which is an evidence that the nature of God is at work in us.

The promise of God stood in relation to Abraham's tried and willing obedience. The revelation of God to us is determined by our character, not by God's (see Psalms 18:25-26). If we are mean, that is how God will appear to us.

By the discipline of obedience we come to the place Abraham reached and see God as He is. The promises of God are of no use to us until by obedience we understand the nature of God. We read some things in the Bible 365 times and they mean nothing to us. Then all of a sudden we see what they mean because in some particular we have obeyed God, and instantly His character is revealed. When with the obedience of our life we say, "Amen—so let it be," to a promise, then that promise is made ours.

The more we have to sacrifice for God, the more glorious will be our reward. We have no right to choose our sacrifice, however. God will let us see what our "Isaac" is to be. God is always at work lifting up the natural and making it the spiritual one. Yet most of us want to cling to the natural when God wants to put a sword through it. If we go through the transfiguration of the natural, we will receive it back on a new plane altogether. God wants to make eternally our own what we only possessed intermittently.

In the beginning we do not train for God, we train for work, for our own aims; but as we go on with God we lose all our own aims and are trained for God's purpose. Unless practical work is appointed by God, it will prove a curse. "At any cost, by any road," means nothing self-chosen.

The Bible does not say God blessed Abraham and took him to heaven, but that He blessed him and kept him on earth. The maturity of character before God is the personal channel through which He can bless others. If it takes our lifetime before God can put us right, then others are going to be impoverished. We need to rise as early as we can and climb our

Mount Moriah, come to the place where God can put an end to the dim gulf between Him and us. Then He will be able to bless us as He did Abraham.

No language can express the affable blessedness of the supreme reward that awaits the soul that has taken its supreme climb, proved its supreme love, and entered on its supreme reward. What an imperturbable certainty there is about the man who is in contact with the real God!… What a depth of transparent "rightness" there must be about the man who walks before God, and the meaning of the Atonement is to place us there in perfect adjustment to God.

—Not Knowing Whither

Questions to Consider
1. How could you cultivate the spirit of obedience in yourself?
2. What is your response to the statement, "To obey is better than sacrifice"?

A Prayerful Response
Lord, give me a spirit that is willing to obey, without thought of the reward. Amen.

THE CALL OF GOD

THOUGHT FOR TODAY

God's call to us is accompanied by the supernatural.

WISDOM FROM SCRIPTURE

Now the word of the LORD came to me saying, "Before I formed you in the womb I knew you, and before you were born I consecrated you; I appointed you a prophet to the nations."

Then I said, "Ah, Lord GOD! Truly I do not know how to speak, for I am only a boy."

But the LORD said to me, "Do not say, 'I am only a boy'; for you shall go to all to whom I send you, and you shall speak whatever I command you. Do not be afraid of them, for I am with you to deliver you, says the LORD."

Then the LORD put out his hand and touched my mouth; and the LORD said to me, "Now I have put my words in your mouth. See, today I appoint you over nations and over kingdoms, to pluck up and to pull down, to destroy and to overthrow, to build and to plant."

The word of the LORD came to me, saying, "Jeremiah, what do you see?" And I said, "I see a branch of an almond tree."

Then the LORD said to me, "You have seen well, for I am watching over my word to perform it."

JEREMIAH 1:4-12, NRSV

INSIGHTS FROM OSWALD CHAMBERS

We are apt to forget the mystic, supernatural touch of God which comes with His call. If a person can tell how the call of

God came and all about it, it is questionable whether he or she ever had the call. The call to be a professional may come in an explicit way, but the call of God is much more supernatural.

The realization of the call of God may come as with a sudden thunderclap or by a gradual dawning, but in whatever way it comes, it arrives with the undercurrent of the supernatural, almost the uncanny. It is always accompanied with a glow—something that cannot be put into words. We need to keep the atmosphere of our minds prepared by the Holy Spirit lest we forget the surprise of God's touch on our lives.

"Before I formed you ... I knew you" (Jeremiah 1:5). There are prenatal forces of God at work in our lives which we may be unconscious of for long enough, but at any moment there may break upon us the sudden consciousness of this incalculable, supernatural, surprising power that has hold of our lives before we have hold of them ourselves.

Another force at work is the prayers of other people. You are born into this world and will probably never know to whose prayers your life is the answer. It may be your father and mother were used by God to dedicate your life to Him before you were born.... Our lives are the answers not only to the prayers of other people, but to the prayer the Holy Spirit is making for us, and to the prayers of our Lord Himself. When once you realize this, you will understand why it is God does not say, "By your leave," when He comes into your life.

If we have been getting hard and metallic, untouched spiritually—not backsliding, but getting out of touch with God—we shall find the reason is that we are allowing things to come in between us and the sense of God's call. At any minute God may bring the wind of His Spirit across our lives, and we shall realize with startled minds that the work we have been doing in the meantime is rubbish (1 Corinthians 3:12-13).

There is so much self-chosen service. We say, "I think I will do this and that for God." Unless we work for God in accordance with His supernatural call, we shall meet havoc and disaster and upset. The moment the consciousness of the call of God dawns on us, we know it is not a choice of our own at all; the consciousness is of being held by a power we do not fully know. Jesus said, "I chose you" (John 15:16)....

"Then Amos answered ... 'I was no prophet, neither was I a son of a prophet, but I was a sheepbreeder, and a tender of sycamore fruit.' Then the Lord took me as I followed the flock, and the Lord said to me, 'Go, prophesy to My people Israel'" (Amos 7:14-15). The only way I can fulfill the call of God is by keeping my convictions out of the way, my convictions as to what I imagine I am fitted for. The fitting goes much deeper than one's natural equipping.

Whenever the call of God is realized, there is the feeling, "I am called to be a missionary." It is a universal feeling because "God so loved the world" (John 3:16). We make a blunder when we fix on the particular location for our service and say, "God called me there." When God shifts the location, the battle comes. Will I remain consistent to what I have said I am going to do, or be true to the insurgent call of God, and let Him locate me where He likes?

The most, seemingly, untoward circumstances will be used by God for the men and women He has called. However much of wrong or of the devil there may seem to be at work, if an individual is called of God, every force will be made to tell for God's purpose in the end. God watches all these things when once we agree with His purpose for us, and He will bring not only the conscious life, but all the deeper regions of life which we cannot reach, into harmony with His purpose. If the call of God is there, it is not within the power of untoward things to turn you. Your heart remains not untouched by them, but unbroken....

We try to make calls out of our own spiritual consecration, but when we are put right with God, He blights all our sentimental convictions and devotional calls. He brushes them aside and rivets us with a terrific passion that is terrific, to one thing we had never dreamed of, and in the condition of real communion with God, we hear Him saying, "Whom shall I send, and who will go for Us?"

And for one radiant, flashing moment we see what God wants, and say in conscious freedom, "Here am I! Send me" (Isaiah 6:8)....

Have we answered God's call in every detail? Have we really been the "sent" ones of Jesus, as He was the sent One of God? What has been competing for our strength? What kind of things have we objected to? What things have hindered our times of communion?...

"Woe unto me," said Paul, "if I do not keep concentrated on this one thing: that I am called of God for His service" (1 Corinthians 9:16, paraphrased).

—So Send I You

QUESTIONS TO CONSIDER
1. How have you heard God's call to spiritual service?
2. How has God's call proved different from your ideas about service?

A PRAYERFUL RESPONSE
Lord, I desire to follow Your call in Your way. Amen.

GOD IS LOVE

THOUGHT FOR TODAY

Love is not an attribute of God; it is God.

WISDOM FROM SCRIPTURE

Dear friends, let us love one another, for love comes from God. Everyone who loves has been born of God and knows God.

Whoever does not love does not know God, because God is love.

This is how God showed his love among us: He sent his one and only Son into the world that we might live through him.

This is love: not that we loved God, but that he loved us and sent his Son as an atoning sacrifice for our sins.

Dear friends, since God so loved us, we also ought to love one another.

No one has ever seen God; but if we love one another, God lives in us and his love is made complete in us.

We know that we live in him and he in us, because he has given us of his Spirit.

And we have seen and testify that the Father has sent his Son to be the Savior of the world.

If anyone acknowledges that Jesus is the Son of God, God lives in him and he in God.

And so we know and rely on the love God has for us. God is love. Whoever lives in love lives in God, and God in him.

In this way, love is made complete among us so that we will have confidence on the day of judgment, because in this world we are like him.

There is no fear in love. But perfect love drives out fear, because fear has to do with punishment. The one who fears is not made perfect in love.

We love because he first loved us.

1 JOHN 4:7-19, NRSV

INSIGHTS FROM OSWALD CHAMBERS

Look back over your own history as revealed to you by grace, and you will see one central fact growing large: God is love. No matter how often your faith in such an announcement was clouded, no matter how the pain and suffering of the moment made you speak in a wrong mood, still this statement has borne its own evidence along with it most persistently. God is love.

In the future, when trials and difficulties await you, do not be fearful. Let not this faith slip from you: God is love. Whisper it not only to your heart in its hour of darkness, but here in the corner of God's earth. Live in the belief of it; preach it by your sweetened, chastened, happy life; sing it in consecrated moments of peaceful joy, sing until the world around you "is wrought to sympathy with hopes and fears it heeded not."

The world does not bid you sing, but God does. Song is the sign of an unburdened heart; so sing your songs of love unbidden, ever rising higher and highest into a fuller concept of the greatest, grandest fact on the stage of life: God is love.

But words and emotions pass, precious as their influence may be for the time; so when the duller moments come and the mind comes to require something more certain and sure to consider than the memory of mere emotions and stirring sentiments, consider this revelation: the eternal fact that God is love—not, God is loving.

God and love are synonymous. Love is not an attribute of God; it is God. Whatever God is, love is. If your concept of love does not agree with justice, judgment, purity, and holiness, then your idea of love is wrong. It is not love you conceive of in your mind, but some vague infinite foolishness, all tears and softness and of infinite weakness.

Though it is too difficult, nay impossible, to trace that God is love by mere unaided human intellect, it is not impossible to the intuitions of faith. Lift up your eyes and look abroad over the whole earth, and in the administration of God's moral government you will begin to discern that God is love; that over sin, war, death, and hell He reigns supreme; that His purposes are ripening fast. We must, by holy contemplation of all we have considered, keep ourselves in the love of God; then we shall not despond for long.

The love of God performs a miracle of grace in graceless human hearts. Human love and lesser loves must wither into the most glorious and highest love of all—the love of God. Then we shall see not only each other's faults, we shall see the highest possibilities in each other and shall love each other for what God will yet make of us. Nothing is too hard for God, no sin too difficult for His love to overcome, not a failure but He can make it a success.

God is love. One brief sentence; it is the gospel. A time is coming when the whole world will know that God reigns and that God is love, when hell and heaven, life and death, sin and salvation, will be read and understood aright at last.

God is love. A puzzle text, to be solved slowly, as with tears and penitence, by prayer and joy, by vision and faith, and last, by death.

—The Love of God

QUESTIONS TO CONSIDER
1. How have you already experienced that God is love?
2. How do you need His love now?

A PRAYERFUL RESPONSE
Lord, I believe You are love and that Your love reigns in my life. Amen.

PART TWO

Pursuing His Holiness

My life is like a faded leaf,
My harvest dwindled to a husk;
Truly my life is void and brief
And tedious in the barren dusk;
My life is like a frozen thing,
No bud nor greenness can I see;
Yet rise it shall—the sap of Spring;
O Jesus, rise in me.

My life is like a broken bowl,
A broken bowl that cannot hold
One drop of water for my soul
Or cordial in the searching cold;
Cast in the fire the perished thing;
Melt and remould it, till it be
A royal cup for him, my King:
O Jesus, drink of me.

❧

Christina Rossetti, "A Better Resurrection"

Oswald Chambers' Insight

Holiness is Christ filling us with His nature
and living through us.

THE IMITATION OF HOLINESS

THOUGHT FOR TODAY

A relationship with Jesus, not religious experience, imparts His holiness to us.

WISDOM FROM SCRIPTURE

Therefore, rid yourselves of all malice and all deceit, hypocrisy, envy, and slander of every kind.

Like newborn babies, crave pure spiritual milk, so that by it you may grow up in your salvation, now that you have tasted that the Lord is good.

As you come to him, the living Stone—rejected by men but chosen by God and precious to him—you also, like living stones, are being built into a spiritual house to be a holy priesthood, offering spiritual sacrifices acceptable to God through Jesus Christ.

For it is commendable if a man bears up under the pain of unjust suffering because he is conscious of God. But how is it to your credit if you receive a beating for doing wrong and endure it? But if you suffer for doing good and you endure it, this is commendable before God.

To this you were called, because Christ suffered for you, leaving you an example, that you should follow in his steps.

"He committed no sin, and no deceit was found in his mouth."

When they hurled their insults at him, he did not retaliate; when he suffered, he made no threats. Instead, he entrusted himself to him who judges justly.

He himself bore our sins in his body on the tree, so that we might die to sins and live for righteousness; by his wounds you have been healed.

For you were like sheep going astray, but now you have returned to the Shepherd and Overseer of your souls.

1 PETER 2:1-5, 19-25, NIV

INSIGHTS FROM OSWALD CHAMBERS

For one child to imitate another child only results in a more or less clever affection; a child imitating his parents assists the expression of inherent tendencies, naturally and simply, because he is obeying a nascent [or natural] instinct. It is to this form of imitation that Peter alludes: ["Leaving us an example, that ye should follow in his steps" (1 Peter 2:21)]. When a saint imitates Jesus, he does it easily because he has the Spirit of Jesus in him.

Pharisaic holiness, both ancient and modern, is a matter of imitation, seeking by means of prayer and religious exercises to establish, seriously and arduously, but un-regeneratedly, a self-determined holiness. The only spiritually holy life is a God-determined life. "Be ye holy; for I am the Lord your God" (Leviticus 20:7). If our best obedience, our most spotless moral walking, our most earnest prayers, are offered to God in the very least measure as the ground of our acceptance by Him, it is a denial of the Atonement....

The only holiness that exists is the holiness derived through faith, and faith is the instrument the Holy Spirit uses to organize us into Christ.... Holiness, like sin, is a disposition, not a series of acts. A man can act holy, but not have a holy disposition. The saint has had imparted to him the disposition of holiness, therefore holiness must be the characteristic of the life here and now. Entire sanctification is the end of the disposition of sin, but only the beginning of the life of a saint. Then comes growth at the moment of birth from above and is consummated on the unconditional surrender of my right to myself to Jesus Christ.

["I beseech you therefore, brethren, by the mercies of God, that ye present your bodies a living sacrifice, holy, acceptable unto God, which is your reasonable service. And be not conformed to this world: but be ye transformed by the renewing of your mind, that ye may prove what is that good, and acceptable, and perfect will of God" (Romans 12:1-2).]

Romans 12:2 is the apostle Paul's passionate entreaty that we rouse ourselves out of the stagnation which must end in degeneration.... "Be ye transformed by the renewing of your mind," says Paul. It is because we have failed to realize that God requires intellectual vigor on the part of the saint that the devil gets his hold on the stagnant mental life of so many. To be transformed by the renewing of our mind means the courageous lifting of all our problems—individual, family, social, and divine—into the spiritual domain, and habitually working out a life of practical holiness there. It is not an easy task, but a gloriously difficult one, requiring the mightiest effort of our human nature, a task which lifts us into thinking God's thoughts after Him.

"That ye may prove what is the good and acceptable and perfect will of God." God's will is only clearly understood by the development of spiritual character; consequently, saints interpret the will of God differently at different times. It is not God's will that alters, but the saint's development in character. Only by intense habitual holiness, by the continual renewing of our mind, and the maintenance of an unworldly spirit, can we be assured of God's will concerning us, even the thing which is "good and acceptable and perfect."

—*Conformed to His Image*

QUESTIONS TO CONSIDER

1. What is your understanding of holiness? How would you define it?
2. How have you pursued holiness?

A PRAYERFUL RESPONSE

Lord, as I grow to know You better, impart Your holiness to me. Amen.

THE MATURE CHRISTIAN

THOUGHT FOR TODAY

Spiritual maturity means bringing the whole life under God's control.

WISDOM FROM SCRIPTURE

[Jesus said,] "If your right eye causes you to sin, gouge it out and throw it away. It is better for you to lose one part of your body than for your whole body to be thrown into hell.

"And if your right hand causes you to sin, cut it off and throw it away. It is better for you to lose one part of your body than for your whole body to go into hell.

"You have heard that it was said, 'Eye for eye, and tooth for tooth.'

"But I tell you, do not resist an evil person. If someone strikes you on the right cheek, turn to him the other also.

"And if someone wants to sue you and take your tunic, let him have your cloak as well.

"If someone forces you to go one mile, go with him two miles.

"Give to the one who asks you, and do not turn away from the one who wants to borrow from you.

"You have heard that it was said, 'Love your neighbor and hate your enemy.'

"But I tell you: Love your enemies and pray for those who persecute you, that you may be sons of your Father in heaven. He causes his sun to rise on the evil and the good, and sends rain on the righteous and the unrighteous.

"If you love those who love you, what reward will you

get? Are not even the tax collectors doing that?

"And if you greet only your brothers, what are you doing more than others? Do not even pagans do that?

"Be perfect, therefore, as your heavenly Father is perfect.

MATTHEW 5:29-30, 38-48, NIV

INSIGHTS FROM OSWALD CHAMBERS

God is so almightily simple that it is impossible to complicate Him, impossible to put evil into Him or bring evil out of Him, impossible to alter His light and love. The nature of the faith born in me by the Holy Spirit will take me back to the Source and enable me to see what God is like. Until I am all light and love in Him, the things in me which are not of that character will have to pass.

In the beginning of Christian experience the life is maimed because we are learning. There is the right eye to be plucked out, the right hand to be cut off, and we are apt to think that is all God means; it is not. What God means is what Jesus said: "Ye shall be perfect, as your heavenly Father is perfect."

When we discern that the sword brought across our natural life is not for destruction, but for discipline, we get His idea exactly. God never destroys the work of His own hands. He removes what would pervert it, that is all. Maturity is the stage at which the whole life has been brought under the control of God.

Psalms 121:1 portrays the "upward look" of a follower of God: "I will lift up my eyes unto the hills, from whence cometh my help. My help cometh from the Lord, which made heaven and earth." The upward look of a mature Christian is not to the hills, but to the God who made the hills. It is the maintained set of the highest powers of a man—not star-gazing till he stumbles, but the upward gaze deliberately set toward God. He is through the "choppy waters" of his elementary spiritual experience and now is set on God....

[Isaiah 33:17 describes the "forward look" of a Christian: "Thine eyes shall see the king in his beauty: they shall behold the land that is very far off."] The forward look is the look that sees everything in God's perspective.... Caleb had the perspective of God; the men who went up with him saw only the inhabitants of the land as giants and themselves as grasshoppers (Numbers 13:33). Learn to take the long view and you will breathe the benediction of God among the squalid things that surround you.

Some people never get ordinary or commonplace; they transfigure everything they touch because they have the forward look which brings their confidence in God out into the actual details of life.... Paul was so identified with Jesus Christ that he had the audacity to say that what men saw in his life in the flesh was the very faith of the Son of God (see Galatians 2:20). Paul is not referring to his own elementary faith in Jesus Christ as his Savior, but to the faith of the Son of God, and he says that that identical faith is now in him.

Fortitude in trial comes from having the long view of God. No matter how closely I am imprisoned by poverty, or tribulation, I see "the land that is very far off" [heaven] and there is no drudgery on earth that is not turned divine by the very sight. Abraham did not always have the forward look; that is why he scurried down to Egypt when there was a famine in the land of promise (see Genesis 12:10).... As soon as I fix on God's "goods," I lose the long view. If I give up to God because I want the hundredfold more, I never see God.

[Isaiah 30:21 presents the "backward look" we are to practice: "And thine ears shall hear a word behind thee, saying, 'This is the way, walk ye in it when ye turn to the right hand, and when ye turn to the left.'"] The surest test of maturity is the power to look back without blinking.

When we look back we get either hopelessly despairing or hopelessly conceited. The difference between the natural backward look and the spiritual backward look is in what we forget. Forgetting in the natural domain is the outcome of vanity: the only things I tend to remember are those in which I figure as being a very fine person! Forgetting in the spiritual domain is the gift of God. The Spirit of God never allows us to forget what we have been, but He does make us forget what we have attained to, which is quite unnatural. The surest sign that you are growing in mature appreciation of your salvation is that as you look back, you never think now of the things you used to bank on before.

Think of the difference between your first realization of God's forgiveness and your realization of what it cost God to forgive you. The hilarity has been merged into holiness. You have become intensely devoted to God who forgave you.

—*Conformed to His Image*

QUESTIONS TO CONSIDER
1. When you look forward and backward on your life, what do you see?
2. How could you adjust this vision to God's viewpoint?

A PRAYERFUL RESPONSE
Lord, teach me to look upward, forward, and backward from Your perspective. Amen.

THE MEMORY OF SIN IN THE SAINT

THOUGHT FOR TODAY

Holiness keeps in mind the personal need for God's redemption.

WISDOM FROM SCRIPTURE

I thank Christ Jesus our Lord, who has given me strength, that he considered me faithful, appointing me to his service.

Even though I was once a blasphemer and a persecutor and a violent man, I was shown mercy because I acted in ignorance and unbelief.

The grace of our Lord was poured out on me abundantly, along with the faith and love that are in Christ Jesus.

Here is a trustworthy saying that deserves full acceptance: Christ Jesus came into the world to save sinners—of whom I am the worst.

But for that very reason I was shown mercy so that in me, the worst of sinners, Christ Jesus might display his unlimited patience as an example for those who would believe on him and receive eternal life.

Brothers, I do not consider myself yet to have taken hold of it. But one thing I do: Forgetting what is behind and straining toward what is ahead, I press on toward the goal to win the prize for which God has called me heavenward in Christ Jesus.

All of us who are mature should take such a view of things. And if on some point you think differently, that too God will make clear to you.

1 TIMOTHY 1:12-16; PHILIPPIANS 3:13-15

No aspect of Christian life and service is more in need of revision than our attitude to the memory of sin in the saint. When the Apostle Paul said "forgetting those things which are behind" (Philippians 3:13), he was talking not about sin, but about his spiritual attainment.

Paul never forgot what he had been; it comes out repeatedly in the Epistles: "For I am the least of the apostles, that am not meet to be called an apostle..." (1 Corinthians 15:9); "Unto me who am less than the least of all saints, is this grace given..." (Ephesians 3:8); "...sinners, of whom I am chief" (1 Timothy 1:15). And these are the utterances of a ripe, glorious servant of God.

If one wants a touchstone for the depth of true spiritual Christianity, one will surely find it in this matter of the memory of sin. There are those who exhibit a Pharisaic holiness: they thank God with an arrogant offensiveness that they are "not as other men are" (Luke 18:11). They have forgotten that horrible pit and miry clay from whence they were taken, and that their feet were set upon a rock through the might of the Atonement.... May the conviction of God come with swift and stern rebuke upon anyone who is remembering the past of another and deliberately choosing to forget his own restoration through God's grace. When a servant of God meets these sins in others, let him be reverent with what he does not understand and leave God to deal with them.

Certain forms of sin shock us far more than they shock God. The sin that shocks God, the sin that broke His heart on Calvary, is not the sin that shocks us. The sin that shocks God is the thing which is highly esteemed among men: self-realization, pride, "my right to myself." We have no right to have the attitude to any man or woman as if he or she had sunk to a lower level than those of us who have never been tempted on the line they have.

The conventions of society and our social relationships make it necessary for us to take this attitude, but we have to remember that in the sight of God there are no social conventions, and that external sins are no worse in His sight than the pride which hates the rule of the Holy Spirit while the life is morally clean. May God have mercy on anyone who forgets this and allows spiritual pride or superiority and a sense of his own unsulliedness to put a barrier between him and those whom God has lifted from the depths of a sin he cannot understand.

Holiness is the only sign that a man is repentant in the New Testament sense, and a holy man is not one who has his eyes set on his own whiteness, but one who is personally and passionately devoted to the Lord who saved him.... Accept as the tender touch of God—not as a snare of the devil—every memory of sin the Holy Spirit brings home to you, keeping you in the place where you remember what you once were and what you now are by His grace....

[Paul said,] "This is a faithful saying, and worthy of all acceptance, that Christ Jesus came into the world to save sinners; of whom I am chief" (1 Timothy 1:15). Sinners, of whom I am chief. What a marvelous humility for a man to say that and mean it!

In the early days of the sterner form of Calvinism a man's belief about God and his own destiny frequently produced a wistful, self-effacing humility. But the humility Paul manifests was produced in him by the remembrance that Jesus, whom he had scorned and despised, whose followers he had persecuted, whose Church he had harried, not only had forgiven him, but made him His chief apostle....

"Howbeit for this cause I obtained mercy, that in me first Jesus Christ might shew forth all long-suffering, for a pattern to them which should hereafter believe on him to life everlasting" (1 Timothy 1:16). Here is the true attitude of the servant of God.... Show such a servant of God the backslider, the sinner steeped in the iniquity of our cities, and there will spring up in his heart an amazing well of compassion and love for that one, because he has himself experienced the grace of God which goes to the uttermost depths of sin and lifts to the highest heights of salvation.

—Conformed to His Image

Questions to Consider

1. How do you feel when remembering your past sins?
2. How can you learn to forget the past, while remembering God's grace toward you?

A Prayerful Response

Lord, thank You for forgiving my sins. Let me not forget Your redemption of me. Help me to extend Your grace to others. Amen.

THE MEANING OF OBEDIENCE

THOUGHT FOR TODAY

Obedience to God is its own reward.

WISDOM FROM SCRIPTURE

And straightway he constrained his disciples to get into the ship, and to go to the other side before unto Bethsaida, while he sent away the people.

And when he had sent them away, he departed into a mountain to pray.

And when even was come, the ship was in the midst of the sea, and he alone on the land.

And he saw them toiling in rowing; for the wind was contrary unto them: and about the fourth watch of the night he cometh unto them, walking upon the sea, and would have passed by them.

But when they saw him walking upon the sea, they supposed it had been a spirit, and cried out: For they all saw him, and were troubled. And immediately he talked with them, and saith unto them, "Be of good cheer: it is I; be not afraid."

And he went up unto them into the ship; and the wind ceased: and they were sore amazed in themselves beyond measure, and wondered.

For they considered not the miracle of the loaves: for their heart was hardened.

MARK 6:45-52, KJV

"And straightway He constrained His disciples to get into the ship, and to go to the other side" (Mark 6:45).

We are apt to imagine that if Jesus Christ constrains us and we obey Him, He will lead us to great success, but He does not. We would have thought these men would have had a successful time, but their obedience led them into a great disaster.

If our Lord has ever constrained you, and you obeyed Him, what was your dream of His purpose? Never put your dream of success as God's purpose for you. His purpose may be exactly the opposite....

The obedience of the disciples led them into great trouble. Jesus did not go with them, a storm came, and they were at their wits' end.... They thought they were going straight to the other side; Jesus knew they would face a storm in the center of the lake.

Each one of us has had similar experiences. We say, "I did obey God's voice. I am sure He led me to do this and that." Yet these very things have led to consternation in our lives. Beware of saying the devil deceived you. It is as true for Christians as for anyone else that "there is a way which seemeth right unto men, but the end thereof are the ways of death" (Proverbs 14:12). We have nothing whatever to do with what men call success or failure. If God's command is clear, and the constraint of His Spirit is clear, we have nothing to do with the result of our obedience.

The purpose of God in calling us is not something in the future, but this very minute.... God's training is for now, not presently, but we have nothing to do with the afterwards of obedience. We get it wrong when we think of the afterwards; the purpose of God is our obedience. Never have a material end in your mind and imagine that God is working toward that by means of your obedience; that is man's way of looking at things.

What man calls training and preparation, God calls the end. The end God has in mind is to enable us to see that He can walk on the chaos of our lives just now.... With how many is the wind contrary these days!

There was no point of rest for the natural mind of the disciples as to what Jesus was after: it was the deep, the dark, and the dreadful. Our Lord's purpose was that they should see Him walking on the sea. We have an idea that God is leading us to a certain goal; He is not. The question of getting to a particular end is a mere incident. "'I know the plans that I am planning for you,' saith the Lord, 'plans of welfare, and not of calamity, to give you an expected end'" (Jeremiah 29:11). What men call the process, God calls the end.

If you can stay in the midst of the turmoil, unperplexed and calm because you see Jesus, that is God's purpose in your life—not that you may be able to say, "I have done this and that and now it's all right." God's purpose for you is that you depend upon Him and His power now; that you see Him walking on the waves, no shore in sight, no success, just the absolute certainty that it is all right because you see Him.

"For they understood not concerning the loaves; for their heart was hardened" (Mark 6:52).

The way our heart is hardened is by sticking to our convictions instead of to Christ. Look back at your life with God, and you will find He has made havoc of your convictions, and now the one thing that looms larger and larger is Jesus Christ and Him only, God and God only. [Jesus prayed,] "And this is life eternal, that they might know Thee the only true God" (John 17:3). Convictions and creeds are *about* God; eternal life is to *know* Him.

...When we dream of ourselves in God's service our hearts do not get troubled: [We say,] "I think this is what God is preparing me for." God is not preparing you for anything; obedience is its own end in the purpose of God. Be faithful to Him. Never say, "I wonder what God is doing with me just now."... The preparation is His end.

Can I see Jesus in my present circumstances? Is it an obscure farther shore, with wild waves between? Can I see Him walking on the waves? Is it a fiery furnace? Can I see Him walking in the midst of the fire? Is it a placid, common-place day? Can I see Him there? If so, that is the perpetual mystery of the guidance of God; that is eternal life.

We have to be transformed by the renewing of our minds, that we may "prove what is the will of God, even the thing which is good and acceptable and perfect" (Romans 12:2) and acceptable and perfect now. If we have a further end in view, we do not pay sufficient attention to the immediate minute. When we know that obedience is the end, then every moment is precious.

—God's Workmanship

QUESTIONS TO CONSIDER
1. What do you think about obedience to God as its own end?
2. What obedience is God asking of you?

A PRAYERFUL RESPONSE
Lord, I desire to obey You, without looking for further reward. Amen.

THINKING GODLINESS

THOUGHT FOR TODAY
Godly thinking requires constant cultivation.

WISDOM FROM SCRIPTURE
Let your gentleness be evident to all. The Lord is near.

Do not be anxious about anything, but in everything, by prayer and petition, with thanksgiving, present your requests to God.

And the peace of God, which transcends all understanding, will guard your hearts and your minds in Christ Jesus.

Finally, brothers, whatever is true, whatever is noble, whatever is right, whatever is pure, whatever is lovely, whatever is admirable—if anything is excellent or praiseworthy—think about such things.

But whatever was to my profit I now consider loss for the sake of Christ.

What is more, I consider everything a loss compared to the surpassing greatness of knowing Christ Jesus my Lord, for whose sake I have lost all things. I consider them rubbish, that I may gain Christ and be found in him, not having a righteousness of my own that comes from the law, but that which is through faith in Christ—the righteousness that comes from God and is by faith.

I want to know Christ and the power of his resurrection and the fellowship of sharing in his sufferings, becoming like him in his death, and so, somehow, to attain to the resurrection from the dead.

PHILIPPIANS 4:5-8; 3:7-11, NIV

In the physical life we do best those things we have habitually learned to do, and the same is true in the mental and spiritual life. We do not come into the world knowing how to do anything; all we do is acquired by habit. Remember, habit is purely mechanical.

Our thinking processes are largely subject to the law of habit.... Self-control is nothing more than a mental habit which controls the body and mind by a dominant relationship: the immediate presence of the Lord—for "the Lord is at hand." The danger in spiritual matters is that we do not think godliness; we let ideas and conceptions of godliness lift us up at times, but we do not form the habit of godly thinking.

Thinking godliness cannot be done in spurts; it is a steady habitual trend. God does not give us our physical habits or our mental habits. He gives us the power to form any habits we like, and in the spiritual domain we have to form the habit of godly thinking.

To a child the universe is a great confusing, amazing "outsideness." When the child grows into an adult, he has the same nervous system and brain, but the will has come in and determined his tendencies and impulses. It is natural for a child to be impulsive, but it is a disgraceful thing for a man or woman to be guided by impulse. To be a creature of impulse is the ruin of mental life. The one thing our Lord checked and disciplined in the disciples was impulse; the determining factor was to be their relationship to Himself....

We have to watch the trend of things. The trend of our conscious life is determined by us, not by God, and Paul makes the determining factor in the conscious life of a godly person the determination to pray. Prayer is not an emotion, not a sincere desire; prayer is a stupendous effort of the will. [Paul advised the Philippians,] "Let your requests be made known unto God. And the peace of God, which passeth all understanding, shall guard your hearts and your thoughts in Christ Jesus" (Philippians 4:7). The poising power of the peace of God will enable you to steer your course in the mix-up of ordinary life.

We talk about "circumstances over which we have no control." None of us have control over our circumstances, but we are responsible for the way we pilot ourselves in the midst of things as they are.... Never allow yourself [to think] that you could not help this or that, and never say you reach anywhere in spite of circumstances. We all attain because of circumstances and no other way.

We have to build up useful associations in our minds, to learn to associate things for ourselves, and it can be done by determination.... For instance, learn to associate the chair you sit in with nothing else but study; associate a selected secret place with nothing but prayer. We do not realize the power we have to infect the places in which we live and work by our prevailing habits.

The law of associated ideas applied spiritually means that we drill our minds in godly connections. How many of us have learned to associate our summer holidays with God's divine purposes? To associate the early dawn with the sunrise on the Sea of Galilee after the Resurrection? If we learn to associate ideas that are worthy of God with all that happens in nature, our imagination will never be at the mercy of our impulses.

Spiritually, it is not a different law that works, but the same law. When once we become accustomed to connecting these things, ordinary occurrences will serve to fructify our minds in godly thinking because we have developed our minds along the lines laid down by the Spirit of God. It is not done once for always; it is only done always.

Never imagine that the difficulty of doing these things belongs peculiarly to you; it belongs to everyone. The character of a person is nothing more than the habitual form of his associations.

...There are people who cultivate the margin of vision; they look at you, but out of the margin of their eyes they are really occupied with something else all the time. In the mental realm there are people who never pay attention to the subject immediately at hand, but only to the marginal subjects round about. Spiritually there is the same danger. Jesus Christ wants us to come to the place where we see things from His standpoint and are identified with His interests only....

Concentration is the law of life mentally, morally, and spiritually.

—*Moral Foundations of Life*

QUESTIONS TO CONSIDER
1. How would you describe your progress toward godly thinking?
2. What godly mental associations can you cultivate today?

A PRAYERFUL RESPONSE
Lord, I will set my mind on You and Your desires. Amen.

Are You Independent or Identified?

Thought for Today

To identify with God is to desire and do His will.

Wisdom from Scripture

Jesus said to them, "Come and have breakfast." None of the disciples dared ask him, "Who are you?" They knew it was the Lord.

Jesus came, took the bread and gave it to them, and did the same with the fish.

This was now the third time Jesus appeared to his disciples after he was raised from the dead.

When they had finished eating, Jesus said to Simon Peter, "Simon son of John, do you truly love me more than these?"

"Yes, Lord," he said, "you know that I love you."

Jesus said, "Feed my lambs."

Again Jesus said, "Simon son of John, do you truly love me?"

He answered, "Yes, Lord, you know that I love you."

Jesus said, "Take care of my sheep."

The third time he said to him, "Simon son of John, do you love me?"

Peter was hurt because Jesus asked him the third time, "Do you love me?" He said, "Lord, you know all things; you know that I love you."

Jesus said, "Feed my sheep.

"I tell you the truth, when you were younger you dressed yourself and went where you wanted; but when you are old you will stretch out your hands, and someone else will dress you and lead you where you do not want to go."

Jesus said this to indicate the kind of death by which Peter would glorify God. Then he said to him, "Follow me!"

JOHN 21:12-19, NIV

INSIGHTS FROM OSWALD CHAMBERS

"Verily, verily, I say unto thee, When thou wast young thou girdest thyself, and walkest whither thou wouldest" (John 21:18).

Jesus is not rebuking Peter; He is revealing a characteristic of us all. Peter had given up everything for the Lord, and the Lord was everything to Peter, but he knew nothing about the "following" that Jesus is referring to. Three years before Jesus had said "Follow Me," and Peter followed easily; the fascination of Jesus was upon him. Then he came to the place where he denied Jesus and his heart broke. Now Jesus says again, "Follow thou Me." Peter follows now in the submission of his intelligence, his will, and his whole being....

When we are young in grace we go where we want to go, but a time comes when Jesus says, "Another shall gird thee" (John 21:18); our will and wish is not asked for. This stage of spiritual experience brings us into fellowship with the Spirit of Jesus, for it is written large over His life that even Christ did not please Himself.

There is a distinct period in our experience when we cease to say, "Lord, show me Thy will," and the realization begins to dawn that we are God's will and He can do with us what He likes. We wake up to the knowledge that we have the privilege of giving ourselves over to God's will. It is a question of being yielded to God.

...When we are young and in grace ... there is a note of independence about our spiritual life: "I don't intend anyone to tell me what to do. I tend to serve God as I choose." It is an independence based on inexperience, an immature fellowship; it lacks the essential of devotion. Some of us remain true to the independent following and never get beyond it; but we are built for God Himself, not for service for God, and that explains the submissions of life. We can easily escape the submissions if we like to rebel against them, but the Spirit of God will produce the most ghastly humiliation if we do not submit.

Since we became disciples of Jesus we cannot be as independent as we used to be.... He expects nothing less than absolute oneness with Himself as He was one with the Father.... Jesus makes us "saints" in order that we may sacrifice our "saintship" to Him, and it is this sacrifice which keeps us one with our Lord.

...[God] will plant us down amongst all kinds of people and give us the amazing joy of proving ourselves "a living sacrifice" in those circumstances (Romans 12:1). "Thou art My beloved Son; in Thee I am well pleased (Matthew 3:17)"; the Father's heart was thrilled with delight at the loyalty of His Son. Is Jesus Christ thrilled with delight at the way we are living a sacrificial life of holiness?...

—Facing Reality

Questions to Consider
1. Do you find joy in sacrifice? Why, or why not?
2. How could you be a living sacrifice in your current circumstances?

A Prayerful Response
Lord, please honor me with the joy of a holy, sacrificial life. Amen.

IRRESISTIBLE DISCIPLESHIP

THOUGHT FOR TODAY

Spiritual strength results more from "standing fast" than from engaging in battle.

WISDOM FROM SCRIPTURE

Finally, be strong in the Lord and in his mighty power.

Put on the full armor of God so that you can take your stand against the devil's schemes.

For our struggle is not against flesh and blood, but against the rulers, against the authorities, against the powers of this dark world and against the spiritual forces of evil in the heavenly realms.

Therefore put on the full armor of God, so that when the day of evil comes, you may be able to stand your ground, and after you have done everything, to stand.

Stand firm then, with the belt of truth buckled around your waist, with the breastplate of righteousness in place, and with your feet fitted with the readiness that comes from the gospel of peace.

In addition to all this, take up the shield of faith, with which you can extinguish all the flaming arrows of the evil one.

Take the helmet of salvation and the sword of the Spirit, which is the word of God.

And pray in the Spirit on all occasions with all kinds of prayers and requests. With this in mind, be alert and always keep on praying for all the saints.

EPHESIANS 6:10-18, NIV

By a "disciple" we mean one who continues to be concentrated on our Lord. *Concentration* is of much more value than *consecration,* because consecration is apt to end in mere religious sentiment.... [Be] "irresistible," not in the sense of being exquisitely charming, or of being irresistible in war, but irresistible in the sense of not being deflected.

...In irresistible discipleship we have to learn an attentive decisiveness. There is a decisiveness that is destructive—a pig-headed decisiveness that decides without deliberation. However, "standing fast in the faith" gives the idea of deliberate, attentive decisiveness. [In other words,] "I will take the time to go through the drill in order to understand what it means to stand fast" (Ephesians 6:13). It is a great deal easier to fight than to stand, but Paul says our conflict is not so much a fight as a standing on guard.

Our Lord requires us to believe very few things because the nature of belief is not mathematical, but something that must be tested—and there are a number of insidious things that work against our faith. A famous preacher said when found in his actual circumstances, he did not believe half so much as he did when he was preaching. He meant he found it difficult to "stand in the faith" in daily circumstances.

It is possible to preach and encourage our own souls and appear to have a very strong faith, while in actual circumstances we do not stand fast at all.... [Someone] said people were trained to think like pagans six days a week and like Christians the remaining day. Consequently, in the actual things of life we decide as pagans, not as Christians at all.

The way of irresistible discipleship is to practice not only alert detachment, but also attentive decisiveness. After having deliberated on the relationship of our faith to certain things, we decide. Jesus said the Holy Spirit would "bring to your remembrance all things whatsoever I have said unto you" (John 14:26). We hear some word of our Lord's and it sinks into the unconscious mind. Then we come into certain circumstances and the Holy Spirit brings back that word to our conscious minds. Are we going to obey our Lord in that particular, or take the ordinary common-sense way of moral decisiveness? Are we going to stand fast in the faith, or take the easier way of decision without deliberation?...

...We have to see that we stand fast in the faith.... "The faith" is faith in the redemption and indwelling Spirit of God: faith that God is love and that He will see after us if we stand steadfast to our confidence in Him. It is easy to stand fast in the big things, but very difficult in the small things. But if we do stand fast in faith in Him, we shall become irresistible disciples.

...If we have been in the habit of discerning the Lord's will and love, and have to decide on the spur of the moment, our determination will be comprehending, that is, we shall decide not from the point of view of self-interest, or because of the good of a cause, but from our Lord's point of view.

One of the finest characteristics of a noble humanity is that of mature patience, not that of impulsive action. It is easy to be determined, and the curious thing is that the more small-minded a man is, the more easily he makes up his mind. If he cannot see the various sides of a question, he decides by the oxlike quality of obstinacy. Obstinacy simply means, "I will not allow any discernment in this matter; I refuse to be enlightened." We wrongly call this strong-mindedness. Strength of mind is the whole mind active, not discernment merely from an individual standpoint....

We can depend on the man or woman who has been disciplined in character, and we become strong in their strength. When we depend on someone who has had no discipline, we both degenerate. We are always in danger of depending on people who are undisciplined, and the consequence is that in the actual strain of life they break down and we do, too. We have to be actually dependable.

When we are young a hurricane or thunderstorm impresses us as being very powerful, yet the strength of a rock is infinitely greater than that of a hurricane. The same is true with regard to discipleship. The strength there is not the strength of activity, but the strength of being.... To convey stability is the work of the Spirit of God....

These considerations convey the characteristics that the Apostle [Paul] wanted the Corinthian Christians to develop in themselves. If we keep practicing, what we practice becomes our second nature; then in a crisis and in the details of life we shall find that not only will the grace of God stand by us, but also our own nature. Whereas if we refuse to practice, it is not God's grace but our own nature that fails when the crisis comes, because we have not been practicing in actual life. We may ask God to help us but He cannot, unless we have made our nature our ally.

The practicing is ours, not God's. He puts the Holy Spirit into us. He regenerates us and puts us in contact with all His divine resources, but He cannot make us walk and decide in the way He wants. We must do that ourselves.

—*Facing Reality*

QUESTIONS TO CONSIDER

1. What do you find more difficult: standing fast or engaging in spiritual battle?
2. How can you increase your ability to stand fast?

A PRAYERFUL RESPONSE

Lord, empower me with the discipline to stand fast in the faith. Amen.

THE MYSTERY OF SANCTIFICATION

THOUGHT FOR TODAY

Sanctification is not striving to be like Christ; it is Christ living through us.

WISDOM FROM SCRIPTURE

Beyond all question, the mystery of godliness is great: He appeared in a body, was vindicated by the Spirit, was seen by angels, was preached among the nations, was believed on in the world, was taken up in glory.

The Spirit clearly says that in later times some will abandon the faith and follow deceiving spirits and things taught by demons.

Such teachings come through hypocritical liars, whose consciences have been seared as with a hot iron.

They forbid people to marry and order them to abstain from certain foods, which God created to be received with thanksgiving by those who believe and who know the truth.

For everything God created is good, and nothing is to be rejected if it is received with thanksgiving, because it is consecrated by the word of God and prayer.

If you point these things out to the brothers, you will be a good minister of Christ Jesus, brought up in the truths of the faith and of the good teaching that you have followed.

Have nothing to do with godless myths and old wives' tales; rather, train yourself to be godly.

For physical training is of some value, but godliness has

value for all things, holding promise for both the present life and the life to come.

This is a trustworthy saying that deserves full acceptance (and for this we labor and strive), that we have put our hope in the living God, who is the Savior of all men, and especially of those who believe.

Command and teach these things.

1 TIMOTHY 3:16-4:11, NIV

INSIGHTS FROM OSWALD CHAMBERS

...If we are going to understand the gospel mystery of sanctification and fully experience it, we must belong to the initiated, that is, we must be born from above by the Spirit of God....

Am I born again of the Spirit of God? What is the relation of my heart to holiness? Our Lord said every tree is known by its fruit and I know whether I am born of the Spirit by the desire of my heart. Do I desire holiness more keenly than I desire any other thing? Do I desire that my motives, my heart, my life, everything in me, should be as pure as God wants it to be? If so, it is a strong witness to the fact I am amongst the mystery of sanctification sufficiently to enter into it.

When we are born again of the Spirit of God, the Word of God awakens great desires in us, and in times of prayer the Spirit renews our minds. In times of meeting with God's people the gracious sense of God's quickening comes until we know the great desire of our hearts before God is to be as holy as God desires us to be. We do want to be baptized with the Holy Spirit so that we bear a strong family likeness to Jesus Christ. These deep desires are strong in the heart of everyone who is born from above....

Do we long for holiness? Are the deepest desires of our

hearts Godward? Do we know, first of all, that we are reconciled to God? Do we know that our sins are forgiven, that God has put the life of His Spirit into us, and are [we] learning how to walk in the light, and are we gaining victories by the power of the Spirit? Do we realize that as we rely on God we have strength to perform our duties in accordance with God's will?...

There is a type of Christian who says, "Yes, I have the desire for holiness. I am reading God's Word; I am trying to be holy and to draw on the resurrection life of Jesus." But never will the mystery of sanctification dawn in that way. It is not God's way....

Another type of Christian says, "Well, I have tried and striven and prayed, but I find it so hard to cut off my right arm, to pluck out my right eye, that I have come to the conclusion that I am unworthy of this great blessing from God. I am not one of those special people who can be holy." I believe there are numbers of Christians who have laid themselves on one side, as it were, and come to the conclusion that sanctification is not meant for them—the reason being that they have tried to work sanctification out their own way instead of God's way, and have failed.

There are others who by strange penances, fastings, prayers, and afflictions to their bodies are trying to work out sanctification. They, too, have tried to penetrate the mystery in a way other than God's appointed way.

Are you trying to work out sanctification in any of these ways? You know that salvation is a sovereign work of grace, but, you say, sanctification is worked out by degrees. God grant that the Spirit of God may put His quiet check on you, and enable you to understand the first great lesson in the mystery of sanctification, which is "Christ Jesus, who of God is made unto us ... sanctification" (1 Corinthians 1:30).

Sanctification does not mean the Lord gives us the ability to produce by a slow, steady process, a holiness like His; *it is His holiness in us....* Whenever Paul speaks of sanctification, he speaks of it as an impartation, never as an imitation. Imitation comes on a different line. Paul does not say, nor does the Spirit of God say anywhere, that after we are born again of the Spirit of God, Jesus Christ is put before us as an example, and that we make ourselves holy by drawing from Him. Never!

Sanctification is Christ formed in us; not the Christ-life, but Christ Himself. In Jesus Christ is the perfection of every-thing, and the mystery of sanctification is that we may have in Jesus Christ, not the start of holiness, but the holiness of Jesus Christ. All the perfections of Jesus Christ are at our dis-posal if we have been initiated into the mystery of sanctifica-tion. No wonder people cannot explain this mystery, for the joy and the rapture and the marvel of it all, and no wonder men see it when it is there, for it works out everywhere.

...The New Testament exhausts itself in trying to expound the closeness of this union. The Spirit of God conveys to the initiated, to those who are born again, what a marvelous thing sanctification is. The perfection of Jesus—ours by the sheer gift of God. God does not give us power to imitate Him: He gives us His very Self.

This is what sanctification means for you and me. Do you say it is too much? Do you know what it comes down to? It comes down to faith: our word is confidence. If we are born again of God by the Spirit, we have not the slightest doubt in our minds of Jesus Christ. We have absolute confidence in Him....

...John the Baptist said of Jesus, "He shall baptize you with the Holy Ghost and with fire" (see Matthew 3:11). The Spirit of God Who wrought out that marvelous life in the

Incarnation will baptize us into the very same life, not into a life like it, but into His life until the very holiness of Jesus is gifted to us. It is not something we work out in Him; it is in Him, and He manifests it through us while we abide in Him. This explains why in the initial stages of sanctification we sometimes see marvelous exhibitions of Christ-like life and patience ... by the baptism of the Holy Ghost the perfections of Jesus are made ours. We are not put into the place where we can imitate Jesus; the baptism of the Holy Ghost puts us into the very life of Jesus.

Are you hungering after sanctification? Have you such confidence in Jesus that you can pray this prayer, the prayer of a child? "Father, in the Name of Jesus, baptize me with the Holy Ghost and fire until sanctification is made real in my life."

—*Our Brilliant Heritage*

QUESTIONS TO CONSIDER
1. What seems mysterious to you about sanctification?
2. Are you hungering for sanctification? Why, or why not?

A PRAYERFUL RESPONSE
Lord, fill me with the Holy Spirit so I live a sanctified life through You. Amen.

THE PHILOSOPHY OF SACRIFICING

THOUGHT FOR TODAY

Jesus Christ grants us the choice to follow Him farther and deeper.

WISDOM FROM SCRIPTURE

Then Jesus said to his disciples, "If anyone would come after me, he must deny himself and take up his cross and follow me.

"For whoever wants to save his life will lose it, but whoever loses his life for me will find it.

"What good will it be for a man if he gains the whole world, yet forfeits his soul? Or what can a man give in exchange for his soul?"

"Come to me, all you who are weary and burdened, and I will give you rest.

"Take my yoke upon you and learn from me, for I am gentle and humble in heart, and you will find rest for your souls.

"For my yoke is easy and my burden is light."

"Come, follow me," Jesus said, "and I will make you fishers of men."

MATTHEW 16:24-26; 11:28-30; 4:19, NIV

INSIGHTS FROM OSWALD CHAMBERS

God does not take the willful "won't" out of us by salvation; at any stage we may say, "No, thank You, I am delighted to be saved and sanctified, but I am not going any farther." Our Lord always prefaced His talks about discipleship with an "if." It has no reference whatever to a soul's salvation or condemnation, but to the discipleship of the personality.

We must bear in mind that our Lord in His teaching reveals unalterable and eternal principles. In Matthew 16:25: "For whosoever would save his life shall lose it: and whosoever shall lose his life for My sake shall find it," Jesus says that the eternal principle of human life is that something must be sacrificed; if we won't sacrifice the natural life, we do the spiritual. Our Lord is not speaking of a punishment to be meted out; He is revealing what is God's eternal principle at the back of human life. We may rage and fret, as men have done, against God's principles, or we may submit and accept and go on, but Jesus reveals that these principles are as unalterable as God Himself.

…In sanctification the freedom of the will is brought to its highest critical point…. It is only then we have a choice; when Jesus Christ emancipates us from the power of sin, that second we have the power to disobey. So this principle…[of choice] works on the threshold of sanctification: "I wonder if I will devote myself to Jesus Christ, or to a doctrine, or to a point of view of my own." Jesus says if we are to be His disciples, we must sacrifice everything to that one thing.

…Christ also said, "Take My yoke upon you [that is, My passion] and ye will find rest unto your souls" (Matthew 11:29). The only place we shall find rest is in the direct education by Jesus in His cross. A new delight springs up in believers who suffer the yoke of Christ. Beware of dissipating that yoke and making it the yoke of a martyr. It is the yoke of a person who owes all he has to the cross of Christ. Paul wore the yoke when he said, "For I am determined not to know anything among you, save Jesus Christ, and Him crucified" (1 Corinthians 2:2). It is the one yoke many people will not wear.

Have I taken the yoke of Christ upon me, and am I walking in the innocent light that comes only from the Spirit of God through the Atonement? When we are born again of the Spirit of God we are made totally new creatures on the inside. That means we live according to the new life of innocence that God has given us, and not be dictated to by the clamoring defects of the temple into which that life has been put. The danger is to become wise and prudent, encumbered with much serving, [for] these things choke the life God has put in [us].

Are we disciples of Jesus? Who is first, or what is first, in our lives? Who is the dominating personality that is dearer to us than life: ourselves or someone else? If it is someone else, who is it?

It is only on such lines that we come to understand what Jesus meant when He said, "If any man would come after Me, let him deny himself" (Matthew 16:24). What He means is that He and what He stands for must be first. The enemies of the Cross of Christ, whom Paul characterizes so strongly, are those who represent the type of things that attract far more than Jesus Christ.... Jesus says, "Die to it all."...

Then said Jesus unto His disciples, "Follow Me" (Matthew 4:19).... [We say,] "We are able." There is no arrogance there, only hopeless misunderstanding. We all say, "Yes, Lord, I will do anything." But will you go to the death of that ... for the noble and true and right? Will you let Jesus take the sense of the heroic right out of you? Will you let Him make you see yourself as He sees you until for one moment you stand before the cross and say, "Nothing in my hands I bring"?

How many of us are there today? ...No crowd on earth

will ever listen to that, and if under some pretense you get them and preach the cross of Christ, they will turn with a snubbing offense from the whole thing as they did in the Lord's day (John 6:60,66)....[But] we must keep true to the cross. Let folks come and go as they will, let movements come and go, let ourselves be swept along or not; the one thing is: [to be] true to the yoke of Christ, His cross.

The one thing we have to stand against is what is stated in Hebrews 12:1: "Therefore let us ... lay aside all cumbrance and the sin which doth so easily beset us," the sin which is admired in many—the sin that gathers round your feet and stops you from running. Get stripped of the whole thing and run with your eye on [Christ].

—If Thou Wilt Be Perfect

QUESTIONS TO CONSIDER
1. What first compelled you to follow Christ?
2. What have you been reluctant to sacrifice for Him?

A PRAYERFUL RESPONSE
Lord, motivate me by Your Spirit to set aside the things that hinder my full surrender to You. Amen.

THE PERFECT LIFE

THOUGHT FOR TODAY

To be "perfect" or complete in Christ, we "sell everything" that possesses us.

WISDOM FROM SCRIPTURE

Now a man came up to Jesus and asked, "Teacher, what good thing must I do to get eternal life?"

"Why do you ask me about what is good?" Jesus replied. "There is only One who is good. If you want to enter life, obey the commandments."

"Which ones?" the man inquired. Jesus replied, "'Do not murder, do not commit adultery, do not steal, do not give false testimony, honor your father and mother,' and 'love your neighbor as yourself.'"

"All these I have kept," the young man said. "What do I still lack?"

Jesus answered, "If you want to be perfect, go, sell your possessions and give to the poor, and you will have treasure in heaven. Then come, follow me."

When the young man heard this, he went away sad, because he had great wealth.

Then Jesus said to his disciples, "I tell you the truth, it is hard for a rich man to enter the kingdom of heaven.

"Again I tell you, it is easier for a camel to go through the eye of a needle than for a rich man to enter the kingdom of God."

When the disciples heard this, they were greatly astonished and asked, "Who then can be saved?"

Jesus looked at them and said, "With man this is impossible, but with God all things are possible."

MATTHEW 19:16-26, NIV

INSIGHTS FROM OSWALD CHAMBERS

After you have entered into life, come and fulfill the conditions of that life. We are so desperately wise, we continually make out that Jesus did not mean what He said and we spiritualize His meaning into thin air. In this case there is no getting out of what He means: "If thou wilt be perfect, go and sell what thou hast, and give to the poor" (Matthew 19:21).

The words mean a voluntary abandonment of property and riches, and a deliberate devoted attachment to Jesus Christ. To you or me Jesus might not say that, but He would say something equivalent over anything we are depending upon…. To the rich young ruler Jesus said, "Loosen yourself from your property because that is the thing that is holding you." The principle is one of fundamental death to possessions while being obliged to use them. "Sell that thou hast…"—reduce yourself till nothing remains but your consciousness of yourself, and then cast that consciousness at the feet of Christ. That is the bedrock of intense spiritual Christianity. The moral integrity of this man made him see clearly what Jesus meant. A man who had been morally twisted would not have seen, but this man's mind was unwarped by moral damage and when Jesus brought him straight to the point, he saw it clearly.

…[You ask,] "Do you mean to say that it is necessary for our soul's salvation to [sell everything]?" Our Lord is not talking about salvation. He is saying, "If thou wilt be perfect."… Remember, the conditions of discipleship are not the conditions for salvation. We are perfectly at liberty to say, "No, thank You, I am much obliged for being delivered from hell, very thankful to escape the abominations of sin, but when it comes to these conditions it is rather too much; I have my own interests in life, my own possessions."

"But when the young man heard that saying, he went away sorrowful; for he had great possessions" (Matthew 19:22).

"Counterpoise" means an equally heavy weight in the other scale. We hear a thing, not when it is spoken, but when we are in a state to listen. Most of us have only ears to hear what we intend to agree with, but when the surgical operation of the Spirit of God has been performed on the inside and our perceiving powers are awakened to understand what we hear, then we get to the condition of this young man.

When he heard what Jesus said he did not dispute it, he did not argue, he did not say, "I fail to perceive the subtlety of Your meaning." He heard it, found he had too big an interest in the other scale, and drooped away from Jesus in sadness, not in rebellion.

...Remember, Jesus did not claim any of the rich young ruler's possessions. He did not say, "Consecrate them to Me."... One of the most subtle errors is that God wants our possessions; they are not of any use to Him. God does not want our possessions; He wants us.

In this incident our Lord reveals His profound antipathy to emotional excitement. The rich young man's powers were in unbewitched working order when Jesus called him to decide. Beware of the "seeking great things for yourself" idea—cold shivers down the back, visions of angels, and visitations from God.... [Jesus comes to us in the ordinariness of life.] He will never take us at a disadvantage, never terrify us out of our wits by some amazing manifestation of His power and then say, "Follow Me."

He wants us to decide when all our powers are in full

working order, and He chooses the moment when the world, not Himself, is in the ascendant. If we chose Him when He was in the ascendant, in the time of religious emotion and excitement, we would leave Him when the moment of the excitement passed. But if we choose Him with all our powers about us, the choice will abide.

"And come and follow Me." It is not only a question of "binding sacrifice with cords to the horns of the altar"; it is a rising in the might of the Holy Ghost, with your feet on the earth but your heart swelling with the love of heaven, conscious that at last you have reached the position to which you were aspiring. How long are some of us who ought to be princes and princesses for God going to be bound up in the show of things?

We have asked in tears, "What lack I yet?" This is the road and no other: "Come and follow Me."

—*If Thou Wilt Be Perfect*

QUESTIONS TO CONSIDER
1. To increase your devotion to Him, what "possessions" might Christ ask you to sell?
2. How would "selling everything" affect you?

A PRAYERFUL RESPONSE
Lord, what would You have me to do? What are the "possessions" that I need to sell? Amen.

MATTERS FOR MATURITY

THOUGHT FOR TODAY

A spiritually mature person is consistent in spiritual battle.

WISDOM FROM SCRIPTURE

For this reason I remind you to fan into flame the gift of God, which is in you through the laying on of my hands.

For God did not give us a spirit of timidity, but a spirit of power, of love and of self-discipline.

So do not be ashamed to testify about our Lord, or ashamed of me his prisoner. But join with me in suffering for the gospel, by the power of God, who has saved us and called us to a holy life—not because of anything we have done but because of his own purpose and grace.

This grace was given us in Christ Jesus before the beginning of time, but it has now been revealed through the appearing of our Savior, Christ Jesus, who has destroyed death and has brought life and immortality to light through the gospel.

And of this gospel I was appointed a herald and an apostle and a teacher.

That is why I am suffering as I am. Yet I am not ashamed, because I know whom I have believed, and am convinced that he is able to guard what I have entrusted to him for that day.

What you heard from me, keep as the pattern of sound teaching, with faith and love in Christ Jesus.

Guard the good deposit that was entrusted to you—guard it with the help of the Holy Spirit who lives in us.

2 TIMOTHY 1:6-14, NIV

"Be not thou therefore ashamed of the testimony of our Lord, nor of me His prisoner; but be thou partaker of the afflictions of the gospel according to the power of God" (2 Timothy 1:8).

This is the message of a veteran soldier to a young soldier. Timothy was constitutionally timid, and Paul had a marvelous solicitude for him, but he never allowed him to give way to self-pity. "Be instant in season, out of season," whether you feel like it or not; whether you feel well or ill, keep at it. It is a fight which means no rest until it issues in a glorious victory for God.

"Be not thou therefore ashamed of the testimony of our Lord."… The testimony of Jesus to Himself is being explained away today; men and women are swerving from the Truth. The power and vigor of the Holy Spirit in lives must go further than the threshold of the experience of being right with God. Bit by bit the battle for God and His truth must be pushed, and the only way to push it is by experiential belief in Jesus Christ's testimony regarding Himself.

If we have been allowing the silting influence of modern tendencies to overcome us, God grant we may rouse ourselves and get back again to the moral and spiritual fighting trim, free from moral nervousness and spiritual timidity, trusting in God and going steadfastly on.

A derelict ship is a danger to other ships, and a derelict in the pulpit or in the Sunday school or in the pew is a desperately dangerous thing to souls on their way through life.

"Nor of me His prisoner." Nowadays loyalty to the saints is scarcely ever thought of. The Apostle Paul is telling Timothy to be loyal to him, and he uses a remarkable phrase, "His prisoner." Yet Paul is always talking about liberty!

Remaining true to Paul would be a real peril to Timothy's personal liberty.

Have some of us changed our church membership because we no longer want to know certain "out-and-out" people? Do we welcome the "out-and-out" saint as we used to, or are we a little bit shocked when we hear the straight testimony of those who are "in prison"?

Some saints have to be ugly in the eyes of the world for a time. The Holy Spirit makes us understand that in spiritual things, it is the "good" that is the enemy of the "best" every time. Jesus said, "If thy right hand offend thee, cut it off, and cast it from thee" (Matthew 5:30). Off goes the right arm, out comes the right eye, and for a while the life is maimed. But slowly and surely God will bring it around to the perfected relationship. When you are in contact with believers in the maimed stage, be loyal to them. Remember the way you had to go.

Intercessory prayer is the test of loyalty. When a man stands out as a "prisoner of the Lord," the saints must garrison him by prayer. If Satan can make a servant of God bow his head in shame because of the testimony of Jesus, or because he knows a "prisoner of Jesus," he will soon succeed in making him disloyal to Christianity altogether.

"But be thou partaker of the afflictions of the gospel." The gospel of God awakens an intense craving in people and an equally intense resentment, and the tendency is to do away with the resentment. Jesus Christ claims that He can remove the disposition of sin from every man; the only testimony worthy of the name of Jesus is that He can make a sinner a saint. The most marvelous testimony to the gospel is a holy man, one whose living experience reveals what God can do.

"According to the power of God." What is the purpose of God? That the historic Jesus should reproduce Himself by the might of His Atonement in everyone who will be close with Him, that is, deny his right to himself and follow Him. It is not that Jesus Christ puts a permeating influence into a man; He stands outside an individual and brings him to a crisis, and by means of that crisis reproduces Himself in him (see Galatians 4:19).

Thank God, it is not only Timothy who had this marvelous counsel of Paul's. We have it, too. And it is not only the counsel of Paul, but of the grand order of heroes right up to the present day—men and women standing for one thing: the testimony of our Lord.

—*God's Workmanship*

Questions to Consider

1. How can you become more consistent in the spiritual battle?
2. What would test your loyalty to other Christians? Why?

A Prayerful Response

Lord, I long to be consistent in my relationship with You and my representation of You to others. Amen.

PART THREE

PRACTICING THE DISCIPLINES

Who would true valour see,
Let him come hither;
One here will constant be,
Come wind, come weather;
There's no discouragement
Shall make him once relent
His first avowed intent
To be a pilgrim.

Hobgoblin nor foul fiend
Can daunt his spirit;
He knows he at the end
Shall life inherit.
Then fancies fly away,
He'll not fear what men say;
He'll labour night and day
To be a pilgrim.

John Bunyan, "The Pilgrim's Song"

OSWALD CHAMBERS' INSIGHT

Spiritual disciplines nurture our intimacy with God and His purposes.

THE DISCIPLINE OF SPIRITUAL TENACITY

THOUGHT FOR TODAY

Spiritual tenacity leads us to God's purposes.

WISDOM FROM SCRIPTURE

God is our refuge and strength, a very present help in trouble.

Therefore we will not fear, though the earth should change, though the mountains shake in the heart of the sea; though its waters roar and foam, though the mountains tremble with its tumult.

There is a river whose streams make glad the city of God, the holy habitation of the Most High.

God is in the midst of the city; it shall not be moved; God will help it when the morning dawns.

The nations are in an uproar, the kingdoms totter; he utters his voice, the earth melts.

The LORD of hosts is with us; the God of Jacob is our refuge.

Come, behold the works of the LORD; see what desolations he has brought on the earth.

He makes wars cease to the end of the earth; he breaks the bow, and shatters the spear; he burns the shields with fire.

"Be still, and know that I am God! I am exalted among the nations, I am exalted in the earth."

The LORD of hosts is with us; the God of Jacob is our refuge.

PSALM 46, NRSV

Tenacity is more than endurance. It is endurance which has at its heart the absolute certainty that what we look for is going to transpire. Spiritual tenacity is the supreme effort of the Spirit of God in a man refusing to believe that his "Hero" is going to be conquered.

The greatest fear a man has is not that he will be damned, but that Jesus Christ will be [defeated]—that the things He stood for—love and justice, forgiveness and kindness among men—won't win out in the end. Then comes the call to spiritual tenacity, not to hang on and do nothing, but to work deliberately and tenaciously with the certainty that God is not going to be [defeated].

There is a wildness all through nature and we are suddenly struck with its brutality and ask, "Why, if God is a beneficent Creator, does He allow such diabolical things to happen?" Has the Bible anything to say about this, any revelation that explains it?

The Bible's explanation is that nature is in a disorganized condition, that it is out of gear with God's purposes and will only become organized when God and man are one (see Romans 7:19).

We all have our problems, something about which we say, "Now, why is it?" Never take an explanation which is too slight. A materialistic explanation or an evolutionary explanation cannot be final. The great thing is to remain absolutely confident in God. "Be still, and know that I am God" (Psalms 46:10).

...In the whirlwind of nations such as is on just now, many a man has lost not his faith in God, but his belief in his beliefs. When a man's belief in his beliefs suffers a severe blow, for a while he thinks he is disbelieving in God. In reality he has lost the conception of God that had been presented to him and he is coming to a knowledge of God along a new line.

There are those who have maintained their faith in God, and the only language they can use to express it is, "I know God is God, although hell seems on top all round."

We are apt to make the mistake of looking for God to put things ostensibly right immediately. If we dwell much on the Second Coming without having a right spiritual relationship to God, it will make us ignore the need for spiritual tenacity.

Just now Jesus says, "The kingdom of God cometh not with observation ... for lo, the kingdom of God is in the midst of you" (Luke 17:21). When our Lord does come, He will come quickly, and we will find He has been there all the time.

One of the greatest strains in life is the strain of waiting for God.... God takes the saint like a bow which He stretches, and at a certain point the saint says, "I can't stand any more." But God does not heed; He goes on stretching because He is aiming at His mark, not ours, and the patience of the saints is that they "hang in" until God lets the arrow fly.

If your hopes are being disappointed just now it means they are being purified. There is nothing noble the human mind has ever hoped for or dreamed of that will not be fulfilled. Don't jump to conclusions too quickly; many things lie unsolved, and the biggest test of all is that God looks as if He is totally indifferent.

Remain spiritually tenacious.

—God's Workmanship

QUESTIONS TO CONSIDER

1. For what problem situation do you need endurance?
2. How can you build your spiritual tenacity amidst this difficulty?

A PRAYERFUL RESPONSE

Lord, I will remain spiritually tenacious, asking that You become my "very present help" during trouble. Amen.

THE TEST OF TRUTH

THOUGHT FOR TODAY

We test our personal and spiritual experiences by God's Word.

WISDOM FROM SCRIPTURE

Indeed, the word of God is living and active, sharper than any two-edged sword, piercing until it divides soul from spirit, joints from marrow; it is able to judge the thoughts and intentions of the heart.

And before him no creature is hidden, but all are naked and laid bare to the eyes of the one to whom we must render an account.

Since, then, we have a great high priest who has passed through the heavens, Jesus, the Son of God, let us hold fast to our confession.

For we do not have a high priest who is unable to sympathize with our weaknesses, but we have one who in every respect has been tested as we are, yet without sin.

Let us therefore approach the throne of grace with boldness, so that we may receive mercy and find grace to help in time of need.

About this we have much to say that is hard to explain, since you have become dull in understanding.

For though by this time you ought to be teachers, you need someone to teach you again the basic elements of the oracles of God. You need milk, not solid food; for everyone who lives on milk, being still an infant, is unskilled in the word of righteousness.

But solid food is for the mature, for those whose faculties

have been trained by practice to distinguish good from evil.

Therefore let us go on toward perfection, leaving behind the basic teaching about Christ, and not laying again the foundation.

HEBREWS 4:12-16; 5:11–6:1, NRSV

INSIGHTS FROM OSWALD CHAMBERS

[Through the Bible] the revelation of God's will has been brought to us in words. The Bible is not a book containing communications from God, it is God's revelation of Himself, in the interest of grace; God's giving of Himself in the limitation of words. The Bible is not a fairy romance to beguile us from the sordid realities of life; it is the divine complement of the laws of nature, of conscience, and of humanity. It introduces us to a new universe of revelation facts not known to unregenerate commonsense.

The only [interpreter] of these facts is the Holy Spirit, and in the degree of our reception, recognition, and reliance on the Holy Spirit will be [the degree of] our understanding. Facts in the natural domain have to be accepted; our explanation of facts is always open to alteration, but you cannot alter facts. The Bible does not simply explain to us a greatest number of facts; it is the only ground of understanding all the facts, that is, it puts into the hand of the Spirit-born [person] the key to the explanation of all mysteries.

In dealing with revelation facts, the aim is not to produce specialists, but to make practical workers in the Bible domain. …But remember, it is essential to be born of the Spirit before we can enter the domain of Bible revelation. The only method of Bible study is to "prove all things," not by intellect, but by personal experience (1 Thessalonians 5:21).

The context of the Bible is our Lord Jesus Christ and a personal relationship to Him. The words of God and the Word of God stand together; to separate them is to render both powerless. An expounder of God's Word is liable to go off at a tangent if he does not remember this stern, undeviating standard of exposition: no individual experience is of value unless it is up to the standard of the Word of God.

The Bible not only tests experience, it tests truth. "I am the truth," said Jesus (John 14:6). Just as the words of God and the Word of God are the counterpart of each other, so the commandments of our Lord and the conduct of His saints are the counterpart of each other; if they are not, then we are "none of His." The test of truth is the revelation of the Son of God in me, not as a divine revelation of the Son of God in me, not as a divine anticipation, but as a delightful activity now. It is perilously possible to praise our Lord as Savior and Sanctifier, yet cunningly blind our hearts to the necessity of His manifesting in our mortal flesh His salvation and sanctification.

The Bible tests all experience, all truth, all authority, by our Lord Himself and our relationship to Him personally. It is the confession of conduct.... The word "confess" means literally that every bit of my bodily life speaks the same truth as our Lord exhibited in the flesh. It is this scriptural scrutiny that reveals the superb standard of the grace of God. Christian experience is possible only when it is a product of the supernatural grace of God at work in our hearts.

—*God's Workmanship*

QUESTIONS TO CONSIDER

1. In the past, what has been your test for truth?
2. How can you "prove" or test all things through the Bible?

A Prayerful Response

Lord, I want to begin "proving all things" through your Word instead of by my thoughts and experiences. Amen.

THE LIVING BIBLE

THOUGHT FOR TODAY

God's children represent the living proof that His words are true.

WISDOM FROM SCRIPTURE

Every generous act of giving, with every perfect gift, is from above, coming down from the Father of lights, with whom there is no variation or shadow due to change.

In fulfillment of his own purpose he gave us birth by the word of truth, so that we would become a kind of first fruits of his creatures.

You must understand this, my beloved: let everyone be quick to listen, slow to speak, slow to anger; for your anger does not produce God's righteousness.

Therefore rid yourselves of all sordidness and rank growth of wickedness, and welcome with meekness the implanted word that has the power to save your souls.

But be doers of the word, and not merely hearers who deceive themselves.

For if any are hearers of the word and not doers, they are like those who look at themselves in a mirror; for they look at themselves and, on going away, immediately forget what they were like.

But those who look into the perfect law, the law of liberty, and persevere, being not hearers who forget but doers who act—they will be blessed in their doing.

If any think they are religious, and do not bridle their tongues but deceive their hearts, their religion is worthless.

Religion that is pure and undefiled before God, the

Father, is this: to care for orphans and widows in their distress, and to keep oneself unstained by the world.

James 1:17-27, NRSV

INSIGHTS FROM OSWALD CHAMBERS

"Why should I believe a thing because it is in the Bible?" That is a perfectly legitimate question. There is no reason why you should believe it; it is only when the Spirit of God applies the Scriptures to the inward consciousness that a man begins to understand their living efficacy. If we try from the outside to fit the Bible to an external standard, or to a theory of verbal inspiration or any other theory, we are wrong. [Jesus warned,] "Ye search the scriptures, because ye think that in them ye have eternal life; and these are they which bear witness of Me; and ye will not come to Me, that ye may have life" (John 5:39-40).

There is another dangerous tendency: that of closing all questions by saying, "Let us get back to the external authority of the Bible." That attitude lacks courage and the power of the Spirit of God; it is a literalism that does not produce "written epistles" but persons who are more or less incarnate dictionaries. It produces not saints but fossils, people without life, with none of the living reality of the Lord Jesus.

There must be the Incarnate Word and the interpreting word, that is, people whose lives back up what up they preach—"written epistles, known and read of all men" (2 Corinthians 3:2). Only when we receive the Holy Spirit and are lifted into a total readjustment to God do the words of God become "quick and powerful" to us. The only way the words of God can be understood is by contact with the Word of God. The connection between our Lord Himself, who is the Word, and His spoken words is so close that to divorce them is fatal. Jesus said, "The words that I speak unto you, they are spirit, and they are life" (John 6:63).

The Bible does not reveal all truth; we have to find out scientific truth and common-sense truth for ourselves. But knowledge of the Truth, our Lord Himself, is only possible through the reception of the Holy Spirit. [Jesus said,] "Howbeit, when He, the Spirit of truth, is come, He will guide you into all truth" (John 16:13).

The Holy Spirit alone makes the Word of God understandable. The regenerating and sanctifying work of the Holy Spirit is to incorporate us into Christ until we are living witnesses to Him. [The preacher] S.D. Gordon put it well when he said, "We have the Bible bound in morocco, bound in all kinds of beautiful leather; what we need is the Bible bound in shoe leather."

That is exactly the teaching of our Lord. After the disciples had received the Holy Spirit they became witnesses to Jesus; their lives spoke more eloquently than their lips—"and they took knowledge of them, that they had been with Jesus" (Acts 4:13).

The Holy Spirit being imparted to us and expressed through us is the manifested exhibition that God can do all that His Word states He can. It is those who have received the Holy Spirit understand the will of God and "grow up into Him in all things" (Ephesians 4:15).... When we have received the Holy Spirit, we learn the first golden lesson of the spiritual life, which is that God reveals His will according to the state of our character (see Psalms 18:25-26).

—*Biblical Ethics*

Questions to Consider

1. How have you been learning to "grow up into Him in all things"?
2. This week, how can you express God's Word through your actions?

A Prayerful Response

Lord, make me a living epistle who expresses Your life and love to others. Amen.

The Discipline of Loneliness

Thought for Today

Solitude with God repairs and prepares our hearts.

Wisdom from Scripture

For God alone my soul waits in silence; from him comes my salvation.

He alone is my rock and my salvation, my fortress; I shall never be shaken.

How long will you assail a person, will you batter your victim, all of you, as you would a leaning wall, a tottering fence?

Their only plan is to bring down a person of prominence. They take pleasure in falsehood; they bless with their mouths, but inwardly they curse.

For God alone my soul waits in silence, for my hope is from him.

He alone is my rock and my salvation, my fortress; I shall not be shaken.

On God rests my deliverance and my honor; my mighty rock, my refuge is in God.

Trust in him at all times, O people; pour out your heart before him; God is a refuge for us.

Those of low estate are but a breath, those of high estate are a delusion; in the balances they go up; they are together lighter than a breath.

Put no confidence in extortion, and set no vain hopes on robbery; if riches increase, do not set your heart on them.

Once God has spoken; twice have I heard this: that power belongs to God, and steadfast love belongs to you, O Lord. For you repay to all according to their work.

PSALM 62, NRSV

The friendship of a soul who walks alone with God is as abiding as God Himself and, in degree, as terrible. What a volume of meaning there is in these words, so simple in statement: "And looking at Jesus as He walked, he said, 'Behold the Lamb of God!'" (John 1:36).

[A man I know] speaks of his wife as his "dear friend." A friend whose contact and whose memory does not make us ever do our best is one in name only. Friendship to a soul undisciplined by loneliness is a precarious sea on which many have been lost, and on whose shores the wrecks of many human hearts lie rotting.

Solitude with God repairs the damage done by the fret and noise and clamor of the world. To have been on the mount with God means that we carry with us an exhilaration, an incommunicable awe. We do not descend to the valley, no matter how low the walk of the feet may have to be, no matter how perplexing the demon-tossed [people] may be around us, no matter if a cross awaits us in the shadows.

[The Old Testament tells us,] "Now it was so, when Moses came down from Mount Sinai [and the two tablets of the Testimony were in Moses' hand when he came down from the mountain], that Moses did not know that the skin of his face shone while he talked with Him" (Exodus 34:29). [And the New Testament says,] "They marveled. And they realized that they had been with Jesus" (Acts 4:13).

The disaster of shallowness ultimately follows the spiritual life that takes not the shining way upon the mount of God. Power from on high has the Highest as its source, and the solitudes of the Highest must never be departed from, or else the power will cease.

Heart, heart, awake! The love that loveth all
Maketh a deeper calm than Horeb's cave:—
God in thee,—can His children's folly gall?
Love may be hurt, but shall not love be brave?
Thy holy silence sinks in dews of balm;
Thou art my solitude, my mountain-calm!

—George MacDonald

Loneliness marks the child of God. In tumult, in trouble, in disaster, in pestilence, in destruction, in fighting with wild beasts, the child of God abides under the shadow of the Almighty.

The child of God who walks alone with Him is not dependent on places and moods, but carries to the world the perpetual mystery of a dignity, unruffled and unstung by insult, untouched by shame and martyrdom.

The culture of the entirely sanctified life is often misunderstood. The discipline of that life consists of suffering, loneliness, patience, and prayer. How many who started with the high ecstasy of vision have ended in the disaster of shallowness! Time, the world, and God fire out the fools. Our Lord was thirty years preparing for three years' service. The modern stamp is three hours of preparation for thirty years of service. John the Baptist and Paul were trained in the massive solitudes of the desert, as are all characters of God's heroic mold.

. . . not in vain His seers
Have dwelt in solitudes and known that God
High up in open silence and thin air
More presently reveals him, having set
His chiefest temples on the mountain-tops,
His kindling altar in the hearts of men,
And these I knew with peace and lost with pain,
Lamented, and in dreams was my desire

For the flood Jordan, for the running sound
And broken glitters of the midnight moon.

—F.W.H. Meyers

In the momentous crisis of entire sanctification and the baptism of the Holy Spirit and fire, all heaven is opened and the soul is drunk with ecstasy. Yet that is but the introduction to a new relationship. Entirely sanctified soul, alone with God, suffering with Jesus, do you hear Him say, "You do not know what you ask. Are you able to drink the cup that I am about to drink, and be baptized with the baptism that I am baptized with?" (Matthew 20:22).

There is a solitude of despair, a solitude of sin—a vast curse, black with the wrath of God, moaning with the pride of hatred—a solitude which is the aftermath of spent vice and exhausted self-love. There is no God in such solitudes, only an exhausting pessimism and a great despair. These solitudes produce the wayward, wandering cries so prevalent among human beings....

But the solitude of the sanctified, the loneliness of the child of God, brings again the glimmering of his Father's feet among the sorrows and the haunts of human beings. And to the broken in heart, to the bound in hereditary prisons, and to the wounded and weak, Jesus our Savior draws near.

—*Christian Disciplines*

QUESTIONS TO CONSIDER
1. What are your thoughts about spending time in solitude?
2. How might you spend time alone with God this week?

A PRAYERFUL RESPONSE
Lord, in solitude refurbish my soul and draw me deeper into Your heart. Amen.

THE DISCIPLINE OF PATIENCE

THOUGHT FOR TODAY

Patience springs from a heart centered on and strengthened by God.

WISDOM FROM SCRIPTURE

The LORD is my light and my salvation; whom shall I fear? The LORD is the stronghold of my life; of whom shall I be afraid?

When evildoers assail me to devour my flesh—my adversaries and foes—they shall stumble and fall.

Though an army encamp against me, my heart shall not fear; though war rise up against me, yet I will be confident.

One thing I asked of the LORD, that will I seek after: to live in the house of the LORD all the days of my life, to behold the beauty of the LORD, and to inquire in his temple.

For he will hide me in his shelter in the day of trouble; he will conceal me under the cover of his tent; he will set me high on a rock.

Now my head is lifted up above my enemies all around me, and I will offer in his tent sacrifices with shouts of joy; I will sing and make melody to the LORD.

Hear, O LORD, when I cry aloud, be gracious to me and answer me!

"Come," my heart says, "seek his face!" Your face, LORD, do I seek.

Do not hide your face from me. Do not turn your servant away in anger, you who have been my help. Do not cast me off, do not forsake me, O God of my salvation!

If my father and mother forsake me, the LORD will take me up.

Teach me your way, O LORD, and lead me on a level path because of my enemies.

Do not give me up to the will of my adversaries, for false witnesses have risen against me, and they are breathing out violence.

I believe that I shall see the goodness of the LORD in the land of the living.

Wait for the LORD; be strong, and let your heart take courage; wait for the LORD!

PSALM 27, NRSV

INSIGHTS FROM OSWALD CHAMBERS

The subject of patience is so largely dealt with in the Bible that it ought to have a much larger place in our Bible studies and talks.

Patience, to most minds, is associated with exhaustion, or with "patients." Consequently, anything robust and vigorous seems to connect itself with all that is impatient and impetuous. Patience is the result of a well-centered strength. To "wait on the Lord" and to "rest in the Lord" is an indication of a healthy, holy faith, while impatience is an indication of unhealthy, unholy unbelief.

[Paul wrote to biblical believers,] "We are bound to thank God always for you … [for] your patience and faith in all your persecutions and tribulations that you endure" (2 Thessalonians 1:3-4). The life of faith is giving over every other "life" but the life of faith. Faith is not an action of the mind, nor of the heart, nor of the will, nor of the sentiment. It is the centering of the entire person in God.

The heroes of faith cataloged in the eleventh chapter of Hebrews were not people who vaguely trusted that somehow good would be the final goal of ill. They were heroes who died "in faith" (11:13)—not faith in a principle, but faith in a Person who promises.

This cloud of witnesses is not a noble army of poets, or dreamers, or thinkers, but a noble army "who through faith subdued kingdoms, worked righteousness, obtained promises, stopped the mouths of lions, quenched the violence of fire, escaped the edge of the sword, out of weakness were made strong, became valiant in battle, turned to flight the armies of the aliens" (Hebrews 11:33-34). These mighty acts were not wrought by diplomacy, but by faith in God, and we are urged to run with patience this same way, by "looking unto Jesus" (12:2).

In dealing with the patience of Christians, the subject naturally unfolds itself into the patience of faith, the patience of hope, and the patience of love. We have already indicated the chief matter in the patience of faith, namely, faith in a Person who promises.

"The testing of your faith produces patience. But let patience have its perfect work, that you may be perfect and complete, lacking nothing" (James 1:3-4).

"When the Son of Man comes, will He really find faith on the earth?" (Luke 18:8).

"Here is the patience and the faith of the saints" (Revelation 13:10).

"Here is the patience of the saints; here are those who keep the commandments of God and the faith of Jesus" (Revelation 14:12).

These passages assuredly serve to indicate how prominent a place patience plays in God's plans for His saints. It brings again prominently to the front what was stated earlier: patience is an indication of strong spiritual health, not of weakness....

[Then there is the patience of hope, as indicated by the following verses:]

"In this hope we were saved.... But if we hope for what we do not see, we wait for it with patience" (Romans 8:24-25).

"Be patient, brethren, until the coming of the Lord.... You also be patient. Establish your hearts" (James 5:7-8).

"I, John, both your brother and companion in the tribulation, and kingdom and patience of Jesus Christ" (Revelation 1:9).

"We do not lose heart.... while we do not look at the things which are seen, but at the things which are not seen. For the things which are seen are temporary, but the things which are not seen are eternal" (2 Corinthians 4:16, 18).

[And finally, there is the patience of love.]

"Now abide faith, hope, love, these three; but the greatest of these is love" (1 Corinthians 13:13).

" ... that the love with which You loved Me may be in them" (John 17:26).

"... that you, being rooted and grounded in love, may be able to comprehend what is the width and length and depth and height—to know the love of Christ which passes knowledge; that you may be filled with all the fullness of God" (Ephesians 3:17-19)....

The patience of the saints, like the patience of our Lord, puts the sovereignty of God over all the saint's career, and because the love of God is shed abroad in our hearts by the Holy Spirit, we choose by our free will what God predestines. For the mind of God, the mind of the Holy Spirit, and the mind of Christians are held together by a oneness of personal, passionate devotion.

—*Christian Disciplines*

QUESTIONS TO CONSIDER

1. What patience do you desire the most: faith, hope, or love?
2. Are you willing to ask God for this patience? Why, or why not?

A PRAYERFUL RESPONSE

Lord, as You see fit, teach me the patience of faith, hope, and love. Amen.

THE DISCIPLINE OF PERIL

THOUGHT FOR TODAY

During difficulties, God can infuse true peace into our hearts.

WISDOM FROM SCRIPTURE

[Jesus said,] "Do not let your hearts be troubled. Believe in God, believe also in me.

"In my Father's house there are many dwelling places. If it were not so, would I have told you that I go to prepare a place for you?

"And if I go and prepare a place for you, I will come again and will take you to myself, so that where I am, there you may be also.

"And you know the way to the place where I am going."

Thomas said to him, "Lord, we do not know where you are going. How can we know the way?"

Jesus said to him, "I am the way, and the truth, and the life. No one comes to the Father except through me.

"If you know me, you will know my Father also. From now on you do know him and have seen him."

"I have said these things to you while I am still with you.

"But the Advocate, the Holy Spirit, whom the Father will send in my name, will teach you everything, and remind you of all that I have said to you.

"Peace I leave with you; my peace I give to you. I do not give to you as the world gives. Do not let your hearts be troubled, and do not let them be afraid."

JOHN 14:1-7, 25-27, NRSV

"Peace I leave with you, My peace I give to you; not as the world gives, do I give to you. Let not your heart be troubled, neither let it be afraid" (John 14:27).

The disciples, like many today, were not in a state to provide their own inner peace. There are times when inner peace is based on ignorance. But when we awake to the heave in threatening billows, inner peace is impossible unless it is received from our Lord. When our Lord spoke in peace, He made peace. His words are spirit and life. Have you ever received what He spoke?

The peace of sins forgiven, the peace of a conscience at rest with God, is not the peace that Jesus imparts. Those are the immediate results of believing and obeying Him, but it is His own peace He gives, and He never had any sins to be forgiven or an outraged conscience to appease. Have you ever received His peace?

When you are right with God, receive your peace by studying … our Lord Himself. It is the peace that comes from looking at His face and remembering the undisturbed condition of the Lord in every set of circumstances. "But we all, with unveiled face, beholding as in a mirror the glory of the Lord, are being transformed into the same image from glory to glory" (2 Corinthians 3:18).

Are you painfully disturbed just now, distracted by waves and billows of God's providential permission, and having turned over the boulders of your belief, you still find no well of peace or joy or comfort—all is barren? Then look up and receive the undisturbed peace of the Lord Jesus Christ. Above and in the facts of war and pain and difficulties He reigns, peaceful.

Reflected peace is the greatest evidence that I am right with God, for I am at liberty to turn my mind to Him. If I am not right with God, I can never turn my mind anywhere but on myself.... We are changed by looking, not by introspection. The source of peace is God, not myself. It never is my peace, but always His; if He withdraws, it is not there.

If I allow anything to hide the face, the countenance, the memory, the consideration of the Lord Jesus from me, then I am either disturbed or I have a false security. [Paul said,] "Consider Him ... lest you become weary and discouraged in your souls" (Hebrews 12:3). Nothing else is in the least like His peace. It is the peace of God which passes all understanding. Are you looking to Jesus just now in the immediate pressing matter and receiving His peace? Then He will flow peace in and through you.

...This kind of peace banishes trouble just now and presently. The Lord says in effect, "Don't let your heart be troubled out of its relationship with Me." It is never the big things that disturb us, but the trivial things. Do I believe that in the circumstances that are apt to bother me just now, Jesus Christ is not perplexed at all? If I do, His peace is mine....

When we confer with Jesus Christ over our lives, all the perplexity goes because He has no perplexity, and our concern is to abide in Him. The reason we get disturbed is that we have not been considering Him. Lay it all out before Him, and in the face of difficulties, bereavement, and sorrow, hear Him say, "Let not your heart be troubled." Let us be confident in His wisdom and His certainty that all will be well....

There are circumstances and difficulties which can only be described as "the thick of it," and in and through all such [difficulties] the Apostle Paul says we are to be "more than conquerors" (Romans 8:37)....

The vocation of a Christian is to be in the thick of it for [Christ's] sake. Whenever Jesus Christ refers to discipleship or

130

suffering, it is always "for My sake." The deep relationship of the saint is a personal one and the reason a saint can be radiant is that he has lost interest in his individuality and has become absolutely devoted to the person of the Lord Jesus Christ.

When a saint puts his or her confidence in the election of God, no tribulation or affliction can ever touch that confidence. When we realize there is no hope of deliverance in human wisdom or in anything we can do, then Paul counsels us to accept the justification of God and to stand true to Christ Jesus. This is the finest cure for spiritual degeneration or for spiritual sulks.

Can we maintain our vocation in the face of every terror? Paul says we can, because he is persuaded that none of these things "shall be able to separate us from the love of God which is in Christ Jesus our Lord" (Romans 8:35).

—*Christian Disciplines*

QUESTIONS TO CONSIDER
1. What circumstances have placed you in "the thick of it"?
2. How can you untrouble your heart and rest in God?

A PRAYERFUL RESPONSE
Lord, as I spend time with You, infuse me with Your peace. Amen.

WHAT'S THE GOOD OF PRAYER?

THOUGHT FOR TODAY
Prayer not only changes circumstances; it changes us.

WISDOM FROM SCRIPTURE
"And whenever you pray, do not be like the hypocrites; for they love to stand and pray in the synagogues and at the street corners, so that they may be seen by others. Truly I tell you, they have received their reward.

"But whenever you pray, go into your room and shut the door and pray to your Father who is in secret; and your Father who sees in secret will reward you.

"When you are praying, do not heap up empty phrases as the Gentiles do; for they think that they will be heard because of their many words.

"Do not be like them, for your Father knows what you need before you ask him.

"Ask, and it will be given you; search, and you will find; knock, and the door will be opened for you.

"For everyone who asks receives, and everyone who searches finds, and for everyone who knocks, the door will be opened.

"Is there anyone among you who, if your child asks for bread, will give a stone?

"Or if the child asks for a fish, will give a snake?

"If you then, who are evil, know how to give good gifts to your children, how much more will your Father in heaven give good things to those who ask him!"

MATTHEW 6:5-8; 7:7-11, NRSV

Only when a man flounders beyond any grip of himself and cannot understand things does he really pray. Prayer is not part of the natural life. By "natural" I mean ordinary, sensible, healthy, worldly-minded life. Some say that a man will suffer in his life if he does not pray. I question it. Prayer is an interruption of personal ambition, and no person who is busy has time to pray. What will suffer is the life of God in him, which is nourished not by food, but by prayer.

If we look on prayer as a means of developing ourselves, there is nothing in it at all, and we do not find that idea in the Bible. Prayer is other than meditation; it develops the life of God in us. When a man is born from above, the life of the Son of God begins in him, and he can either starve that life or nourish it.

Prayer nourishes the life of God. Our Lord nourished the life of God in Him by prayer; He was continually in contact with His Father. We generally look upon prayer as a means of getting things for ourselves, whereas the biblical idea of prayer is that God's holiness, purpose, and wise order may be brought about. Our ordinary views of prayer are not found in the New Testament.

When a man is in real distress he prays without reasoning; he does not think things out, he simply spurts it out. [In the Old Testament it says,] "Then they cried unto the Lord in their trouble, and he saved them out of their distresses"(Psalms 107:13). When we get into a tight place our logic goes to the winds, and we work from the implicit part of ourselves.

[Matthew 6:8 says,] "Your Father knoweth what things ye have need of, before ye ask him." Then why ask? Very evidently our ideas about prayer and Jesus Christ's are not the same. Prayer to Him is not a way to get things from God, but so that we may get to know God. Prayer is not to be used as the privilege of a spoiled child seeking ideal conditions to indulge his spiritual propensities; the purpose of prayer is to reveal the presence of God, equally present at all times in every condition.

A man may say, "Well, if the Almighty has decreed things, why need I pray? If He has made up His mind, what is the use of my thinking I can alter His mind by prayer?" We must remember that there is a difference between God's order and God's permissive will. God's order reveals His character: His permissive will applies to what He permits. For instance, it is God's order that there should be no sin, no suffering, no sickness, no limitation, no death. His permissive will is all these things. God has so arranged matters that we are born into His permissive will, and we have to get at His order by prayer....

In His teaching about prayer, our Lord never referred to unanswered prayer; He said God always answers prayer. If our prayers are in the name of Jesus, or in accord with His nature, the answers will not be in accord with our nature but with His. We are apt to forget this and to say without thinking that God does not always answer prayer. He does every time, and when we are in close communion with Him we realize we have not been misled....

Be yourself exactly before God and present your problems—the things you have come to your wit's end about. Ask what you will, and Jesus Christ says your prayers will be answered. We can always tell whether our will is in what we ask by the way we live when we are not praying.

The New Testament view of a Christian is someone in whom the Son of God has been revealed, and prayer deals with the nourishment of that life. It is nourished by refusing to worry over anything, for worry means there is something over which we cannot have our own way.... Jesus Christ says,

"Don't worry about your life, don't fear them that kill the body; be afraid only of not doing what the Spirit of God indicates to you" (Matthew 10:28).

...Never let anything push you to your wit's end, because you will get worried, and worry makes you self-interested and disturbs the nourishment of the life of God. Give thanks to God that He is there, no matter what is happening.... The secret of Christian quietness is not indifference, but the knowledge that God is my Father, He loves me, I shall never think of anything He will forget. Worry becomes an impossibility.

It is not so true that "prayer changes things" as that prayer changes us, and then we change things. Consequently we must not ask God to do what He has created us to do. For instance, Jesus Christ is not a social reformer. He came to alter us first, and if there is any social reform to be done on earth, we must do it. God has so constituted things that prayer alters the way we look at things. Prayer is not altering things externally, but working wonders within our disposition. When we pray, things remain the same, but we begin to be different. The same thing [happens] when we fall in love; the circumstances and conditions are the same, [but] we have a sovereign preference in our heart that transfigures everything. If we have been born from above and Christ is formed in us, instantly we begin to see things differently: "If any man be in Christ, he is a new creature" (2 Corinthians 5:17).

...We are never what we are in spite of our circumstance, but because of them. [Someone] once said, "Circumstances are like feather beds—very comfortable to get on top of, but immensely smothering if they get on top of you." Jesus Christ, by the Spirit of God, always keeps us on top of our circumstances.

—If Ye Shall Ask

QUESTIONS TO CONSIDER
1. What situation tempts you to worry about your life?
2. How can you pray for this circumstance?

A PRAYERFUL RESPONSE
Lord, thank You that You will hear and answer my prayers.
Amen.

PRAYING IN THE HOLY SPIRIT

THOUGHT FOR TODAY

When we pray in the Holy Spirit, He teaches us how to pray and what to say.

WISDOM FROM SCRIPTURE

Finally, be strong in the Lord and in the strength of his power.

Put on the whole armor of God, so that you may be able to stand against the wiles of the devil.

For our struggle is not against enemies of blood and flesh, but against the rulers, against the authorities, against the cosmic powers of this present darkness, against the spiritual forces of evil in the heavenly places.

Therefore take up the whole armor of God, so that you may be able to withstand on that evil day, and having done everything, to stand firm.

Stand therefore, and fasten the belt of truth around your waist, and put on the breastplate of righteousness.

As shoes for your feet put on whatever will make you ready to proclaim the gospel of peace.

With all of these, take the shield of faith, with which you will be able to quench all the flaming arrows of the evil one.

Take the helmet of salvation, and the sword of the Spirit, which is the word of God.

Pray in the Spirit at all times in every prayer and supplication. To that end keep alert and always persevere in supplication for all the saints.

EPHESIANS 6:10-18, NRSV

We have to pray relying upon what has been revealed by the sent-down Holy Spirit, and the first revelation is that we do not know how to pray. We have to learn to draw on our relationship with Jesus Christ. As we do, we realize the Holy Spirit keeps us in a simple relationship to our Lord while we pray.

When we pray in the Holy Spirit, we are released from our petitions. [Jesus taught,] "Your Father knoweth what things ye have need of, before ye ask Him" (Matthew 6:8). Then why ask? The whole meaning of prayer is that we may know God. The "asking and receiving" prayer is elementary; it is the part of prayer we can understand. But it is not necessarily praying in the Holy Spirit.

Those who are not born again must ask and receive, but when we have received salvation and have become rightly related to God, we must maintain this simplicity of belief in Him while we pray. Our minds can be saturated by the revelation of prayer until we learn in every detail to pray in the Holy Spirit. Prayer is not an exercise, it is life.

A great many people do not pray because they do not feel any sense of need. We come across people who try us, and all these things awaken a dumb sense of need, which is a sign that the Holy Spirit is there. If we are ever free from the sense of need, it is not because the Holy Spirit has satisfied us, but because we have been satisfied with as much as we have.... A sense of need is one of the greatest benedictions because it keeps our life rightly related to Jesus Christ.

When we learn to pray in the Holy Spirit, we find there are some things for which we cannot pray; we sense a need for restraint. Never push and say, "I know it is God's will and I am going to stick to it." Beware. Remember the children of Israel: "He gave them their request; but sent leanness into their soul" (Psalm 106:15). Let the Spirit of God teach you what He is driving at and learn not to grieve Him. If we are abiding in Jesus Christ, we shall ask what He wants us to ask, whether we are conscious of doing so or not (John 15:7).

When we pray relying on the Holy Spirit, He will bring us back to this one point: we are not heard because we are not in earnest, or because we need to be heard, or because we will perish if we are not heard. We are heard on the ground of the Atonement of the Lord (Hebrews 10:19).

The efficacy of the atoning work of Christ is the one thing the Holy Spirit works into our understanding. As He interprets the meaning of that work to us, we learn never to bank on our own earnestness or on our sense of need. We never have the idea that God does not answer; we become restfully certain that He always does.

The Holy Spirit will continually interpret to us that the only ground of our approach to God is the blood of Jesus. As we learn the spiritual culture of praying in the Holy Spirit, we find that God uses the common-sense circumstances He puts us in, and the common-sense people His providence places us among, to help us realize that the one fundamental thing in prayer is the atoning work of Jesus Christ.

When we pray in the Holy Spirit we begin to have a more intimate conception of God. The Holy Spirit brings all through us the sense of His resources. For instance, the Holy Spirit may call us to a definite purpose for our life and we know that it means a decision, a reckless flinging over onto God, a burning of our bridges behind us, and there is not a soul to advise us when we take that step—except the Holy Spirit.

Our clingings come on this way: We put one foot on God's

side and one on the side of human reasoning. Then God widens the space until we either drop between or jump to one side. We have to take a leap—a reckless leap—and if we have learned to rely on the Holy Spirit, it will be a reckless leap to God's side. So many of us limit our praying because we are not reckless in our confidence in God. In the eyes of those who do not know God, it is madness to trust Him, but when we pray in the Holy Spirit we begin to realize the resources of God, that He is our perfect heavenly Father and we are His children....

Praying in the Holy Spirit gives us insight into why Paul said we wrestle not against flesh and blood, but against principalities and powers, against spiritual wickedness in high places (see Ephesians 6:12). If the Holy Spirit is having His way in us, He will charge the atmosphere round about us. There are things that have to be cleared away by the Holy Spirit. Never fight; stand and wrestle.

Wrestling is not fighting; it is confronting the antagonist on our own ground and maintaining a steady, all-embracing "stand" and "withstand." How many of us succumb to the flesh-and-blood circumstances: "I did not sleep well" or "I have indigestion" or "I did not do quite right there." Never allow any of these things to be your reason for not prevailing in prayer. Hundreds of people with impaired bodies pray in the Holy Spirit.

In work for God, never look at flesh and blood causes; meet every arrangement for the day in the power of the Holy Spirit. It makes no difference what your work is or what your circumstances are. If you are praying in the Holy Spirit, He will produce an atmosphere round about you, and all these things will result in the glory of God.

"Pray without ceasing" (1 Thessalonians 5:17). Keep the childlike habit of continually exclaiming in your heart to God, recognize and rely on the Holy Spirit all of the time. Inarticulate prayer, the impulsive prayer that looks so futile, is the thing God always heeds.

—If Ye Shall Ask

QUESTIONS TO CONSIDER
1. What does praying in the Holy Spirit mean to you?
2. How can you cultivate this type of prayer?

A PRAYERFUL RESPONSE
Lord, teach me to pray without ceasing, and to pray in sync with the Holy Spirit. Amen.

Make a Habit of Having No Habits

Thought for Today

God asks us to focus on Him instead of on our religious habits.

Wisdom from Scripture

May grace and peace be yours in abundance in the knowledge of God and of Jesus our Lord.

His divine power has given us everything needed for life and godliness, through the knowledge of him who called us by his own glory and goodness.

Thus he has given us, through these things, his precious and very great promises, so that through them you may escape from the corruption that is in the world because of lust, and may become participants of the divine nature.

For this very reason, you must make every effort to support your faith with goodness, and goodness with knowledge, and knowledge with self-control, and self-control with endurance, and endurance with godliness, and godliness with mutual affection, and mutual affection with love.

For if these things are yours and are increasing among you, they keep you from being ineffective and unfruitful in the knowledge of our Lord Jesus Christ.

For anyone who lacks these things is nearsighted and blind, and is forgetful of the cleansing of past sins.

Therefore, brothers and sisters, be all the more eager to confirm your call and election, for if you do this, you will never stumble.

For in this way, entry into the eternal kingdom of our Lord and Savior Jesus Christ will be richly provided for you.

2 PETER 1:2-11, NRSV

"For as these qualities exist and increase with you, they render you active and fruitful in the knowledge of our Lord Jesus Christ" (2 Peter 1:8, Moffat).

When we are forming a habit we are conscious of it, but in the real Christian life habits do not appear, because by practice we do things unconsciously. As Christians, we have to learn the habit of waiting upon God as He comes to us through the moments.... When we realize that God's order comes to us in the haphazard, our life will manifest itself in the way our Lord indicates in the Sermon on the Mount.

The illustrations our Lord uses there are "the fowls of the air," "the lilies of the field." Birds and flowers [are not self-conscious]; it is not their own thought that makes them what they are, but the thought of the Father in heaven. If our child-like trust in God is giving place to self-consciousness and self-deprecation, it is a sign that in the place where every habit is so practiced there is no conscious habit at all. Watch how God will upset our programmes if we are in danger of making our little Christian habits our god. Whenever we begin to worship our habit of prayer or Bible reading, God will break up that time. We say, "I cannot do this, I am praying. It is my hour with God." No, it is our hour with our habit; we pray to a habit of prayer.

"For as these qualities exist and increase with you." Are they existing in us? There are times when we are conscious of becoming virtuous and patient and godly, but they are only stages. If we stop there we get the strut of the "pi" [pious] person. A "pi" person is one who does his level best to be what he would like to be, but knows he is not. Our Christian life continually resolves itself into consciousness and introspection because there are some qualities we have not added yet. Ultimately, the relationship is to be a simple one....

Consciousness of a defect is a disease spiritually, yet it is produced by the finger of God because we have neglected to add some quality...patience, godliness, love. We have to exercise the quality until the habit is merged into the simplicity of a child's life.

We have to beware of singling out one quality only. Peter says "as these qualities"—faith, virtue, knowledge, temperance, patience, godliness, brotherly kindness, charity—"exist and increase with you."... [Jesus says,] "Come unto Me and I will give you rest," the rest of perfection of activity that is never conscious of itself (Matthew 11:28). This perfection of activity can be illustrated by the spinning of a colored top. If the top spins quickly, all the colors merge and a musical sound is heard. But if it spins slowly, it wobbles and sighs and every color is conspicuous.

If we are conscious of a defect it is because the Lord is pointing out there is a quality to be added, and until it is added, we are conscious of a black streak here, a colored streak there. But when the particular quality has been added we are no longer conscious of the defect. All the qualities are merged and the whole life is at rest in the perfection of activity.

The dominant thing about a Christian is not self-realization, but the Lord Himself. Consequently, a believer can always be ignored because, to the majority of eyes, our Lord is no more noticeable in the life of a saint than He was to people in the days of His flesh. But when a crisis comes, the saint is the one to whom men turn, and the life which seemed colorless is seen as the white light of God.

"They render you active and fruitful." It is a mistake to fix our eyes on our own "whiteness," for all we are conscious for then is passionate longing for a holy relationship with God.

We have to come to the place where conscious holiness ceases to be because [it has been replaced by] the presence of the One who is holiness. When we have been made partakers of the divine nature we are taken up into God's consciousness; we do not take God into our consciousness.

If we are consciously holy we are far from simple in certain relationships, for there will be certain things we imagine we cannot do, whereas in reality we are the only ones who ought to be able to do those things.

Once we come into a simple relationship with God, He can put us where He pleases and we are not even conscious of where He puts us. All we are conscious of is an amazing simplicity of life that seems to be a haphazard life externally. The only supernatural life ever lived on earth was the life of our Lord, and He was at home with God anywhere.

Whenever we are not at home with God, there is a quality to be added [to our character]. We have to let God press through us in that particular until we gain Him, and life becomes the simple life of a child in which the vital concern is putting God first.

"In the knowledge of our Lord Jesus Christ." ... Knowledge is faith perfected, and faith in turn passes into sight. We experience knowledge until knowledge is swallowed up in the fact of God's presence.... Knowledge is an expression of the nature of God and is the practical outcome of the life of God in us, but if we isolate knowledge we are in danger of criticizing God.

We look for God to manifest Himself to His children. God only manifests Himself in His children; consequently, others see the manifestation, the child of God does not. You say, "I am not conscious of God's blessing now." Thank God! "I am not conscious now of the touches of God." Thank God! "I am not conscious now that God is answering my prayers."

145

Thank God! If you are conscious of these things, it means you have put yourself outside of God.

"That the life also of Jesus might be made manifest in our mortal flesh."... When a little child becomes conscious of being a child, the child-likeness is gone. And when a saint becomes conscious of being a saint, something has gone wrong. We say, "Oh, but I'm not good enough." You never will be good enough! That is why the Lord had to come and save you.... Let God be all in all, and life will become the simple life of a child in which God's order comes moment by moment.

Never live on the memories. Do not remember in your testimony what you once were. Let the Word of God be always living and active in you, and give the best you have every time, all the time.

—Our Brilliant Heritage

QUESTIONS TO CONSIDER

1. Have your religious habits become more important to you than God Himself? How do you know?
2. If so, how can you become less concentrated on these habits?

A PRAYERFUL RESPONSE

Lord, I do not want my spiritual habits to grow more important to me than You. Amen.

PART FOUR

REACHING OUR WORLD

Lord, it belongs not to my care,
Whether I die or live;
To love and serve thee is my share,
And this thy grace must give.

If life be long I will be glad,
That I may long obey;
If short — yet why should I be sad
To soar to endless day?

Christ leads me through no darker rooms
Than he went through before;
He that unto God's kingdom comes,
Must enter by this door.

~

Richard Baxter, "Lord, It Belongs Not to My Care"

OSWALD CHAMBERS' INSIGHT
God's work is accomplished when we use His ways to do it.

HOW TO THINK ABOUT OTHER PEOPLE

THOUGHT FOR TODAY

God asks us to pattern ourselves after Him and love one another.

WISDOM FROM SCRIPTURE

One of the teachers of the law came and heard them debating. Noticing that Jesus had given them a good answer, he asked him, "Of all the commandments, which is the most important?"

"The most important one," answered Jesus, "is this: 'Hear, O Israel, the Lord our God, the Lord is one. Love the Lord your God with all your heart and with all your soul and with all your mind and with all your strength.'

"The second is this: 'Love your neighbor as yourself.' There is no commandment greater than these."

"Well said, teacher," the man replied. "You are right in saying that God is one and there is no other but him. To love him with all your heart, with all your understanding and with all your strength, and to love your neighbor as yourself is more important than all burnt offerings and sacrifices."

When Jesus saw that he had answered wisely, he said to him, "You are not far from the kingdom of God." And from then on no one dared ask him any more questions....

When [Judas] was gone, Jesus said, "Now is the Son of Man glorified and God is glorified in him. If God is glorified in him, God will glorify the Son in himself, and will glorify him at once.

"My children, I will be with you only a little longer. You will look for me, and just as I told the Jews, so I tell you now: Where I am going, you cannot come.

"A new command I give you: Love one another. As I have loved you, so you must love one another.

"By this all men will know that you are my disciples, if you love one another."

MARK 12:28-34; JOHN 13:31-35, NIV

INSIGHTS FROM OSWALD CHAMBERS

"A new commandment I give unto you, that ye love one another; as I have loved you, that ye also love one another" (John 13:34).

There is no subject more intimately interesting to people than man's relationship to man, but men get impatient when they are told that the first requirement is that they should love God first and foremost. The first of all the commandments is, "Thou shalt love the Lord thy God with all thy heart, and with all thy soul, and with all thy mind, and with all thy strength; this is the first commandment" (Mark 12:30).

In every crisis in our lives, is God first in our love? In every perplexity of conflicting duties, is He first in our leading?

"And the second is like, namely this, 'Thou shalt love thy neighbor as thyself'" (verse 31). Remember the standard, "as I have loved you." I wonder where the best of us are according to that standard? How many of us have turned away over and over again in disgust at men, and when we get alone with the Lord Jesus He speaks no word, but the memory of Him is quite sufficient to bring the rebuke, "as I have loved you."

It takes severe training to think habitually along the lines Jesus Christ has laid down, although we act on them impulsively sometimes.

How many of us are letting Jesus Christ take us into His school of thinking? The Christian who is thoughtful is like a man fasting in the midst of universal intoxication. Men of the world hate a thoughtful believer. They can ridicule a living saint who does not think, but a thinking saint—I mean, of course, one who lives rightly as well—is an annoyance, because the thinking saint has formed the mind of Christ and re-echoes it.

Let us from this time forth determine to bring into captivity every thought to the obedience of Christ. Let us love one another.

—Biblical Ethics

QUESTIONS TO CONSIDER

1. Is there someone you particularly need to love as Christ loved you?
2. If so, how, specifically, can you begin to love this person as Christ loved you?

A PRAYERFUL RESPONSE

Lord, I desire to love others as You have loved me. Show me how to love them. Amen.

THE KEY TO SERVICE

THOUGHT FOR TODAY

Prayer is the key to accomplishing the "greater works" God asks us to do.

WISDOM FROM SCRIPTURE

Jesus went through all the towns and villages, teaching in their synagogues, preaching the good news of the king-dom and healing every disease and sickness.

When he saw the crowds, he had compassion on them, because they were harassed and helpless, like sheep with-out a shepherd.

Then he said to his disciples, "The harvest is plentiful but the workers are few. Ask the Lord of the harvest, therefore, to send out workers into his harvest field."

He called his twelve disciples to him and gave them authority to drive out evil spirits and to heal every disease and sickness.

"Believe me when I say that I am in the Father and the Father is in me; or at least believe on the evidence of the miracles themselves.

"I tell you the truth, anyone who has faith in me will do what I have been doing. He will do even greater things than these, because I am going to the Father.

"And I will do whatever you ask in my name, so that the Son may bring glory to the Father.

"You may ask me for anything in my name, and I will do it.

"If you love me, you will obey what I command.

"And I will ask the Father, and he will give you another

Counselor to be with you forever—the Spirit of truth. The world cannot accept him, because it neither sees him nor knows him. But you know him, for he lives with you and will be in you."

—MATTHEW 9:35–10:1; JOHN 14:11-17, NIV

INSIGHTS FROM OSWALD CHAMBERS

Prayer is usually considered to be devotional and more or less impractical in ordinary life. Our Lord in His teaching always considered prayer work, not preparation for work.

Thank God for all the marvelous organization there is in Christian work: for medical missions and finely educated missionaries, for aggressive work in every shape and form. But [in regard to the key to service,] these [organizations] are only pieces of the lock. The key is not in any of our organizations; the key lies in our hand by the Lord's instruction, "Pray ye therefore" (Matthew 9:38).

[Jesus also said,] "Verily, verily I say unto you, He that believeth on me, the works that I shall do he shall do also; and greater works than these shall he do; because I go unto my Father. And whatsoever ye ask in my name, that will I do, that the Father may be glorified in the Son" (John 14:12-13).

Have the "greater works" been done? They certainly have. These men our Lord said these words to wrote the New Testament, and the reason they wrote it was that the Lord, when He was glorified, sent forth the personal Paraclete, the Holy Spirit, not only in His power—His power and influence were at work before Pentecost—but He sent Him forth to this earth personally where He is to this hour, and through His might and inspiration produced the "greater works," namely, the New Testament.

But what does it mean for us?... The great basis of prayer is to realize we must take orders from our Master. He puts all the emphasis on prayer, and He made prayer not preparation for the work, not a sentiment or a devotion, but the work. There is real danger of worshiping prayer instead of praying because we worship....

We pray on the great fundamental basis of redemption, and our prayers are made efficient by the wonderful presence of the personal Holy Spirit in the world. Prayer is simple, prayer is supernatural, and to anyone not related to our Lord Jesus Christ, prayer is apt to look stupid. It sounds unreasonable to say God will do things in answer to prayer, yet our Lord said that He would. Our Lord bases everything on prayer. Then the key to all our work as Christians is, "Pray ye therefore."

When we pray for others the Spirit of God works in the unconscious domain of their being [in a way] that we know nothing about and the one we are praying for knows nothing about. But after the passing of time, the conscious life of the one prayed for begins to show signs of unrest and disquiet.... If we have been praying, we find that on meeting them one day there is the beginning of a softening and a desire to know something.

It is that kind of intercession that does the most damage to Satan's kingdom. It is so light, so feeble in its initial stages, that if our reason is not wedded to the light of the Holy Spirit, we will never do it. Yet it is that kind of intercession the New Testament places the most emphasis on....

It seems stupid to think we can pray and [such things] will happen, but remember to whom we pray. We pray to a God who understands the unconscious depths of personality about which we know nothing, and He has told us to pray. The great Master of the human heart said, "Greater works than these shall ye do ... and whatsoever ye ask in my name, that will I do" (John 14:12-13).

Not only is prayer the work, but prayer is the way fruit abides. Our Lord put prayer as the means to fruit-producing and fruit-abiding work; but remember, it is prayer based on His agony, not ours. "Ye have not chosen me, but I have chosen you, and ordained you, that ye should go and bring forth fruit, and that your fruit should remain; that whatsoever ye shall ask of the Father in my name; he may give it to you" (John 15:16).

Prayer is not only the work and the way fruit abides, but prayer is the [spiritual] battle.... Do we remember to pray on the ground of our Lord's orders for all who minister in His name? If the Apostle Paul earnestly solicited prayer on his behalf that he might "make known with boldness the mystery of the Gospel" (Ephesians 6:19), surely we should remember that this is the key our Lord puts into our hands for all Christian work. Not prayer because we are helpless, but prayer because God is almighty.

Jesus did not say, "Go into the field." He said, "Pray ye therefore the Lord of the harvest." That does not so much mean the harvest is the world; it means that there are innumerable people who have reached a crisis in their lives—they are "white already to harvest." We find them everywhere, not only in foreign countries, but in neighboring houses, and the way we discern who they are is not by intellect, not by suggestions, but by prayer.

"Pray ye therefore." Prayer is labor, not agony, but labor on the ground of our Lord's redemption in simple confidence in Him. Prayer is simple to us because it cost Him so much to make it possible. God grant that we may work victories for Him by taking His way about it.

—If Ye Shall Ask

155

Questions to Consider

1. Are you laboring in prayer before you engage in spiritual work? Why, or why not?
2. How can you arrange more time for prayer?

A Prayerful Response

Lord, before I engage in spiritual work, I will labor in prayer for the harvest. Amen.

THE GOD=APPROVED WORKER

THOUGHT FOR TODAY

God-approved workers are careful of what they listen to and what they say.

WISDOM FROM SCRIPTURE

Remember Jesus Christ, raised from the dead, descended from David. This is my gospel, for which I am suffering even to the point of being chained like a criminal. But God's word is not chained.

Therefore I endure everything for the sake of the elect, that they too may obtain the salvation that is in Christ Jesus, with eternal glory.

Here is a trustworthy saying: If we died with him, we will also live with him; if we endure, we will also reign with him. If we disown him, he will also disown us; if we are faithless, he will remain faithful, for he cannot disown himself.

Keep reminding them of these things. Warn them before God against quarreling about words; it is of no value, and only ruins those who listen.

Do your best to present yourself to God as one approved, a workman who does not need to be ashamed and who correctly handles the word of truth.

Avoid godless chatter, because those who indulge in it will become more and more ungodly.

… God's solid foundation stands firm, sealed with this inscription: "The Lord knows those who are his," and, "Everyone who confesses the name of the Lord must turn away from wickedness."

2 TIMOTHY 2:8-16, 19, NIV

"Be diligent to present yourself approved to God, a worker who does not need to be ashamed, rightly dividing the word of truth" (2 Timothy 2:15).

...How can a man or woman become a worker approved to God? Read 1 Timothy 4:16: "Take heed to yourself, and to the doctrine." If you forget everything else, do not forget that verse. The word "heed" occurs also in Acts 3:5 and 20:28. It means to concentrate—to screw your mind down, fix it, limit it, curb it, confine it, rivet it on yourself and your teaching. It is a strong word, a powerful word, a word that grips, a rousing word. That is what we have to do if we are going to be workers approved to God.

But ... notice who is talking and who he is talking to. It is the Apostle Paul talking to Timothy, or writing to Timothy, or sending a message to Timothy. Paul's method was that of apprenticeship—that is always God's method of training workers. In the old days when artists used to have apprentices, they used to put the young person in charge of mixing paints and, in between this, the younger one would watch the artist paint. Slowly, bit by bit, doing the hard work and watching the master work, [the young person] would learn to "take heed."

That was Paul's method. Timothy had a good mother and a godly grandmother, and he was trained spiritually in this apprentice style. If you are going to be a worker for the care of souls, God will bring you under masters and teachers. That is the method God always uses. He does not use anyone who is undisciplined. Thank God for every worker who was ever placed under apprenticeship!...

There are two kinds of [spiritual] workers—the one who may become a castaway; that is what the Apostle Paul dreaded. [He said,] "I discipline my body and bring it into subjection, lest, when I have preached to others, I myself should become disqualified" (1 Corinthians 9:27). The other kind of worker is the one who is an example of what he or she teaches.... "Search after that kind of preacher, Timothy," [said Paul,] "and listen to that one."

Worker for God ... what do you fasten your mind on when you listen to a preacher, when you read a book? When Jesus Christ said, "You shall love the Lord your God with all your heart," He did not stop there. He continued: "with all your soul, with all your mind, and with all your strength" (Mark 12:30).... Would to God we had the same stick-to-it energy in God's line! Many have I known in Scotland who worked hard day and night to attain scholarships in secular callings, and are we to be behind them? This word of the Apostle Paul's is used in that connection: concentrate, stick at it, fix the mind on it. Give heed to reading, be careful of your self-preparation. God grant that we may be approved to God by what we build in [to us]....

Paul said to Timothy another thing: "Remind them of these things, charging them before the Lord not to strive about words to no profit, to the ruin of the hearers" (2 Timothy 2:14). And again, "Shun profane and idle babblings, for they will increase to more ungodliness. And their message will spread like cancer" (verses 16-17). And again, "Avoid foolish and ignorant disputes, knowing that they generate strife" (verse 23).

Don't argue! Don't enter into controversy at any price.... Paul spent most of his days in controversy, and yet he told Timothy not to argue! But have you read Paul's method of controversy? Paul put himself with amazing courtesy and amazing insight and amazing tenderness into the place of the person he was disputing with. The reason Paul told Timothy not to argue, and the reason he tells me not to argue, and the reason he tells you not to argue, is that we argue from our own point of view. We argue not for the truth's sake; we argue to prove we are right. God grant that we may learn to take heed lest we get switched off on arguing....

"Heal me," prayed Augustine again and again, "of this lust of mine of always vindicating myself."

Take heed, fix your mind, never be wheedled into controversy. Let the Spirit of God controvert. One of my greatest snares since I became a Christian is this very thing. I know what it means. I know the galling humiliation and agony of wanting to argue the point out and I know... the inwardness of the point that the Apostle Paul is driving at with Timothy: "Don't do it, Timothy. Stop, you will damage your own soul. You will hinder the Truth of God. You will bruise the souls you talk to." God grant we may fix and concentrate our minds and take heed to this!

Take heed to yourself, take heed how you read, and above all, don't argue. Have you learned this, Christian worker?...

—Workmen of God

QUESTIONS TO CONSIDER

1. How can you respond to the advice, "Take heed to yourself"?
2. How do you feel about the advice, "Don't argue"? How can you apply it to your life?

A PRAYERFUL RESPONSE

Lord, I will "take heed" over what information enters my mind and what words exit from my mouth. Amen.

A PASSION FOR SOULS

THOUGHT FOR TODAY

A passion for souls spills from a passionate relationship with God.

WISDOM FROM SCRIPTURE

Yet when I preach the gospel, I cannot boast, for I am compelled to preach. Woe to me if I do not preach the gospel!

If I preach voluntarily, I have a reward; if not voluntarily, I am simply discharging the trust committed to me.

What then is my reward? Just this: that in preaching the gospel I may offer it free of charge, and so not make use of my rights in preaching it.

Though I am free and belong to no man, I make myself a slave to everyone, to win as many as possible.

To the Jews I became like a Jew, to win the Jews. To those under the law I became like one under the law (though I myself am not under the law), so as to win those under the law.

To those not having the law I became like one not having the law (though I am not free from God's law but am under Christ's law), so as to win those not having the law.

To the weak I became weak, to win the weak. I have become all things to all men so that by all possible means I might save some.

I do all this for the sake of the gospel, that I may share in its blessings.

Do you not know that in a race all the runners run, but only one gets the prize? Run in such a way as to get the prize.

Everyone who competes in the games goes into strict training. They do it to get a crown that will not last; but we do it to get a crown that will last forever.

1 CORINTHIANS 9:16-25, NIV

INSIGHTS FROM OSWALD CHAMBERS

You hear people say that Paul showed his wonderful breadth of mind, his culture and generosity, his gentleness and patience, by becoming all things to all people. He did nothing of the sort. He said, "I have become all things to all men" for one purpose only—"that I may by all means save some" (1 Corinthians 9:22).

He did not say, "I became all things to all men that I might show what a wonderful human being I am." There is no thought of himself in the matter.

The phrase "a passion for souls" is a dangerous one; a passion for souls may be either a diseased lust or a divine life. Let me give you a specimen of it as a diseased lust: "Woe to you, scribes and Pharisees, hypocrites! For you travel land and sea to win one proselyte, and when he is won, you make him twice as much a son of hell as yourselves" (Matthew 23:15).

"Proselyte" is a technical word for convert, and our Lord is showing that these Pharisees had a great passion for a soul which He stamped as of the devil. If you read the thirteenth chapter of Acts, you will find a remarkable thing occurred. The proselytes became exactly what Jesus Christ said they would: "twice as much a son of hell" and far more superstitious and fanatical. The devout women alluded to who persecuted the apostles: the proselytes (Acts 13:43-50)....

But have we got clearly in our minds what the passion for souls as a divine life is? Read James 5:19-20: "Brethren, if anyone among you wanders from the truth, and someone turns him back, let him know that he who turns a sinner from the error of his way will save a soul from death and cover a multitude of sins." The apostle is talking to those whom we understand [to be] Christians: "If anyone among you, brethren, wanders from the truth."

Again our Lord in speaking to His disciples used some striking phrases, all of which refer to this passion of souls. In Matthew 4:18-22, He spoke about making them "fishers of men." In John 21:15-17, He said, "Feed My sheep"—a striking phrase which has a direct bearing on the right passion for souls. After the Resurrection He said, "Go therefore and make disciples of all the nations" (Matthew 28:16-20)....

There is a telling pathos about the twenty-first chapter of John. All the disciples had forsaken the Shepherd, and Jesus said, in effect, "Now, never you forsake the flock; you become broken bread and poured out wine and feed the flock." God grant we may understand that the passion for souls is no placid, scientifically worked out thing. It is a consuming, fiery, living passion.

Take ... the phrase, "fishers of men." There are one or two significant things about that figure of speech. The early disciples were fishermen, and the Spirit of God seems to point out that their earthly employment was a parable of their divine vocation. David was a shepherd; he became the shepherd of Israel. Paul was a tentmaker; he was used by God for making people's bodies into tabernacles of the Holy Spirit.

I wonder how many of you know what it is to be out all night at sea fishing? I do. Before the early dawn, about three or four in the morning, you feel so amazingly cold and so amazingly indifferent that you don't know whether you care for anything, and there is an exact counterpart of those nights in work for God. Do you know what it is to have a relationship to God so consuming, a personal, passionate devotion to Jesus Christ so powerful, that it will stand you in good stead through every cold night while you are watching and waiting to land individuals for God? It is those cold nights of waiting that are the test. Cold nights of praying and preaching when, like Gideon's army over again, many leave and forsake, and just the few are left.

What a marvelous illustration fishing is! Especially fishing with the net. Jesus Christ told the disciples He would make them fishers of men, catchers of human souls. Unless we have this divine passion for souls burning in us because of our personal love for Jesus Christ, we will quit the work before we are much older. It is an easy business to be a fisherman when you have all the enthusiasm of the catch; everybody then wants to be a fisherman ... but God is wanting those who, through long nights, through difficult days of spiritual toil, have been trying to let down their nets to catch the fish.

Oh the skill, the patience, the gentleness, and the endurance that are needed for this passion for souls. A sense that people are perishing doesn't do it; only one thing will do it: a blazing passion, a devotion to the Lord Jesus Christ, an all-consuming passion. Then there is no night so long, no work so hard and no crowd so difficult, but that love will outlast it all.

...May we see our passion for souls spring from [the Scripture] on which the Moravian Mission founded its enterprise: Isaiah 53. Behind every face besotted with sin, they saw the face of the Son of God. Behind every broken piece of earthenware, they saw Jesus Christ. Behind every downtrodden mass of human corruption they saw Calvary. That was the passion that was their motive.... That is the deep, true evangelical note for the passion for souls—the consuming passion that transfigures a man's self, that transfigures a woman's self, and makes him or her indeed wise and patient and an able fisher for human souls.

Beware of the people who tell you how to fish! I know a good many people who have tried to learn how to fish from books, but they never did learn. The only way to learn how to fish is to fish! An old sea captain who I know very well, who has been a fisherman all his days, told me he met a man who had published a book on how to catch fish. The captain took him out in his boat for four hours, but [the author] didn't have enough strength to put one piece of line over the boat—he was too seasick....

Beware of books that tell you how to "catch" people. Go to Calvary and let God Almighty deal with you, until you understand the tremendous cost to our Lord Jesus Christ. Then go out to catch humans. God grant that we may get away from the instructors on how to catch fish and get out into the fishing business!

—Workmen of God

Questions to Consider

1. How might you increase your passion for Christ?
2. Do you feel compelled to bring people to Him? Why, or why not?

A Prayerful Response

Lord, please fill me with a passion to capture souls for You. Amen.

THE WORKER'S SPIRITUAL LIFE

THOUGHT FOR TODAY

Be careful: religious experience can replace a relationship with Christ.

WISDOM FROM SCRIPTURE

I have been crucified with Christ and I no longer live, but Christ lives in me. The life I live in the body, I live by faith in the Son of God, who loved me and gave himself for me.

I do not set aside the grace of God, for if righteousness could be gained through the law, Christ died for nothing!

You foolish Galatians! Who has bewitched you? Before your very eyes Jesus Christ was clearly portrayed as crucified.

I would like to learn just one thing from you: Did you receive the Spirit by observing the law, or by believing what you heard?

Are you so foolish? After beginning with the Spirit, are you now trying to attain your goal by human effort?

Have you suffered so much for nothing—if it really was for nothing?

Does God give you his Spirit and work miracles among you because you observe the law, or because you believe what you heard?

Consider Abraham: "He believed God, and it was credited to him as righteousness." Understand, then, that those who believe are children of Abraham.

The Scripture foresaw that God would justify the Gentiles by faith, and announced the gospel in advance to Abraham: "All nations will be blessed through you."

So those who have faith are blessed along with Abraham, the man of faith.

All who rely on observing the law are under a curse, for it is written: "Cursed is everyone who does not continue to do everything written in the Book of the Law."

Clearly no one is justified before God by the law, because, "The righteous will live by faith."

The law is not based on faith; on the contrary, "The man who does these things will live by them."

Christ redeemed us from the curse of the law by becoming a curse for us, for it is written: "Cursed is everyone who is hung on a tree."

He redeemed us in order that the blessing given to Abraham might come to the Gentiles through Christ Jesus, so that by faith we might receive the promise of the Spirit.

GALATIANS 2:20–3:14, NIV

INSIGHTS FROM OSWALD CHAMBERS

As a worker [for God,] watch the "sea-worthiness" of your spiritual life; never allow spiritual leakage. Spiritual leakage arises either by refusing to treat God seriously, or by refusing to do anything for Him seriously. Bear in mind two things: the pressure of God on your thought from without, and the pressure of God on your attention from within....

There are three ways we can reasonably receive communication from God: 1) by giving deliberate, thoughtful attention to the Incarnation; 2) by identifying ourselves with the Church; 3) by means of Bible revelation. God gave Himself in the Incarnation; He gives Himself to the Church; He gives Himself in His Word. These are the ways He has ordained for conveying His life to us.

The mere reading of the Word of God has power to

communicate the life of God to us mentally, morally, and spiritually. God makes the words of the Bible a sacrament, that is, the means whereby we partake of His life. It is one of His secret doors for the communication of His life to us.

Our whole being, not one aspect of it, has to be brought to comprehend the love of God. We are apt to coordinate our spiritual faculties only; our lack of coordination is detected if we cannot pass easily from what we call the secular to the sacred. Our Lord passed from the one to the other without any break. The reason we cannot is that we are not pressed on to the life of God; we have made "a world within the world" of our own which we have to guard jealously. [We say,] "I must not do this and that. I must keep myself entirely here."

That is not the life of God at all; it is not genuine enough; it is artificial and cannot stand the strain of actual life. There is no room in the New Testament for sickly piety, only for the robust, vigorous, open-air life that Jesus lived—in the world but not of it, the whole life guided and transfigured by God. Beware of the piety that is not stamped by the life of God, but by a type of religious experience.

Be absolutely and fiercely godly in your life, but never be pious. A "pi" person does not take God seriously, he only takes himself seriously. The one tremendous worship of his life is his experience.

If we would concentrate on God, we must mortify our religious self-will. Our Lord refused to be self-willed religiously, and it was this that staggered the Pharisees. We are self-willed religiously; consequently, we tell God we do not intend to concentrate on Him, we only intend to concentrate on our idea of what the "saintly life" should be. Before long we find that the pressing in of the life of God ceases and we begin to wilt. We are living a religiously self-centered life and the communication of life from God comes no longer. We must be aware of turning away from God by grubbing our own experiences.

God does not expect us to imitate Jesus Christ: He expects us to allow the life of Jesus to be manifested in our mortal flesh. God engineers circumstances and brings us into difficult places where no one can help us, and we can either manifest the life of Jesus in those conditions, or be cowards and say, "I cannot exhibit the life of God there." Then we deprive God of glory.

If you will let the life of God be manifested in your particular human edition ... you will bring glory to God. The spiritual life of a worker is literally "God manifest in the flesh" (1 Timothy 3:16).

—*Approved Unto God*

Questions to Consider

1. In what new way can you learn to listen to God: the Incarnation, the Church, the Bible?
2. How can you break down barriers between the sacred and secular in your life?

A Prayerful Response

Lord, I want my spiritual life to draw from You, not from religious experiences. Amen.

WHERE AM I SPIRITUALLY?

THOUGHT FOR TODAY

If we let them, trials bring us into a right relationship with God.

WISDOM FROM SCRIPTURE

Dear friends, do not be surprised at the painful trial you are suffering, as though something strange were happening to you.

But rejoice that you participate in the sufferings of Christ, so that you may be overjoyed when his glory is revealed.

If you are insulted because of the name of Christ, you are blessed, for the Spirit of glory and of God rests on you.

If you suffer, it should not be as a murderer or thief or any other kind of criminal, or even as a meddler.

However, if you suffer as a Christian, do not be ashamed, but praise God that you bear that name.

For it is time for judgment to begin with the family of God; and if it begins with us, what will the outcome be for those who do not obey the gospel of God?

And, "If it is hard for the righteous to be saved, what will become of the ungodly and the sinner?"

So then, those who suffer according to God's will should commit themselves to their faithful Creator and continue to do good.

Humble yourselves, therefore, under God's mighty hand, that he may lift you up in due time.

Cast all your anxiety on him because he cares for you.

1 PETER 4:12-19; 5:6-7, NIV

The Christian worker must be sent; he must elect to go. Nowadays that is the last thing thought of; it is a determination on the part of the individual. He says, "This is something I can do, and I am going to do it." Beware of demanding that people go into work; it is a craze. The majority of saved souls are not fit to feed themselves yet.

How am I to know I have been sent of God? First, by the realization that I am utterly weak and powerless and if I am to be of any use to God, He must do it all of the time. Is this the humiliating certainty of my soul, or merely a sentimental phrase?

Second, because I know I have to point men to Jesus Christ, not to get them to think what a holy person I am. The only way to be sent is to let God lift us right out of any sense of "fitness" in ourselves, and place us where He will. The man whose work "tells for God" is the one who realizes his utter "unfitness" and overwhelming unsuitability—the impossibility of God ever calling [him]. God allows us to scrutinize ourselves to understand what Paul said: "We also are weak in Him" (2 Corinthians 13:4).

Occasionally it may happen in your life as a worker that all you have been trying honestly and eagerly to do for God falls about your ears in ruins, and in your utterly crushed and discouraged condition God brings slowly to your mind this truth: "I have been using your work as scaffolding to perfect you to be a worker for Myself. Now arise, shake off the dust, and I will tell you what you must do."

Before ever God can use us as workers, He has to bring us to a place of entire poverty, where we shall have no doubt as to where we are: "Here I am, absolutely no good!" Then God can send us, but not until then. We put hindrances in the way of God's working by trying to do things for Him.

The impatience of modern life has so crept into Christian work that we will not settle down before God and find out what He wants us to do.

No one can tell you where the shadow of the Almighty is [see Psalms 91:1]; you must find that out for yourself. When you have found out where it is, stay there. Under the shadow no evil can ever befall you. The intensity of the moments spent under the shadow of the Almighty is the measure of your usefulness as a worker. Intensity of communion is not in feelings or emotions or in special places, but in quiet, fixed, confident centering on God. Never allow things to hinder you from being in the place where your spiritual life is maintained.

The expression of our lips must correspond with our communion with God. It is easy to say good and true things without troubling to live up to them. Consequently, the "Christian talker" is more likely to be a hypocrite than any other kind of worker. In all probability you will find that you could express things better a few months or years ago than you can now, because the Spirit of God has been asking you to realize since then what you are talking about....

Peter [talks] about suffering, and he says, "The time is come that judgment must begin at the house of God" (1 Peter 4:17). Where is the house of God? My body.... An undisciplined Christian is inclined either to despise the chastening and say it is of the devil, or else to faint when he is rebuked, and cave in.

The writer to the Hebrews said, "If you are a saint you will be chastened. Be careful, see that you don't despise it." Or it may be suffering as Jesus suffered (see Hebrews 5:8; 2 Corinthians 1:5). In all these ways we have to learn how to let judgment begin at the house of God. We try to escape judgment in a hundred and one ways; consequently, we do not develop [spiritually]....

If you are a worker whom God has sent, and have learned to live under His shadow, you will find that scarcely a day goes by without your Father revealing the need for further chastening. If any child of God is free from the goads of God, he is not in the line of the succession of Jesus Christ. If we suffer as He suffered, we are in the right line (see 1 Peter 4:13).

We have to learn to bring the scrutiny of God's judgment upon ourselves. When we talk about suffering, we are apt to think only of bodily pain, or of suffering because we have given up something for God, which is paltry nonsense. Joy and peace and delight come into the life of the Christian, but they are so on the surface that he never heeds them. They are simply complements [to being right with God].

The one central point for the saint is being absolutely right with God, and the only way he gets there is by this personal experience of judgment.

—Approved Unto God

Questions to Consider
1. How might God be using difficult circumstances to change you?
2. How can you learn to accept and not fight God's judgments in your life?

A Prayerful Response
Lord, thank You that trials can bring me closer to You. Amen.

KEEP IT SIMPLE

THOUGHT FOR TODAY

Faith grows when we live according to the gospel's simplicity.

WISDOM FROM SCRIPTURE

You are looking only on the surface of things. If anyone is confident that he belongs to Christ, he should consider again that we belong to Christ just as much as he.

For even if I boast somewhat freely about the authority the Lord gave us for building you up rather than pulling you down, I will not be ashamed of it.

I do not want to seem to be trying to frighten you with my letters.

For some say, "His letters are weighty and forceful, but in person he is unimpressive and his speaking amounts to nothing."

Such people should realize that what we are in our letters when we are absent, we will be in our actions when we are present.

We do not dare to classify or compare ourselves with some who commend themselves. When they measure themselves by themselves and compare themselves with themselves, they are not wise.

We, however, will not boast beyond proper limits, but will confine our boasting to the field God has assigned to us, a field that reaches even to you.

We are not going too far in our boasting, as would be the case if we had not come to you, for we did get as far as you with the gospel of Christ.

Neither do we go beyond our limits by boasting of work done by others. Our hope is that, as your faith continues to grow, our area of activity among you will greatly expand, so that we can preach the gospel in the regions beyond you. For we do not want to boast about work already done in another man's territory.

But, "Let him who boasts boast in the Lord."

For it is not the one who commends himself who is approved, but the one whom the Lord commends.

I hope you will put up with a little of my foolishness; but you are already doing that.

I am jealous for you with a godly jealousy. I promised you to one husband, to Christ, so that I might present you as a pure virgin to him.

But I am afraid that just as Eve was deceived by the serpent's cunning, your minds may somehow be led astray from your sincere and pure devotion to Christ.

2 Corinthians 10:7–11:3, NIV

INSIGHTS FROM OSWALD CHAMBERS

There must be two centers to our mental life as [spiritual] workers: the first is personal faith in Jesus Christ; the second, personal reliance on the human reason that God made. Most of us think from one center only, the center of human reason. Consequently, all that Jesus Christ stands for beyond the reach of human reason is ignored.

"I fear," says Paul, "lest . . . your minds should be corrupted from the simplicity that is in Christ" (2 Corinthians 11:3). Beware of making simple what the Bible does not. The line of our simplicity is in Christ: "I am the way, the truth, and the life" (John 14:6). The way the simplicity that is in Christ is corrupted is by trying to live according to a statement made by men's heads. [Our relationship with

God] must be the relationship of a child [and a Father] all through (see Matthew 11:25). To be able to state explicitly in words what you know by faith is an impossibility; if you can state it in words, it is not faith.

The way the serpent beguiled Eve was by enticing her away from personal faith in God to depend on her reason alone. Confusion comes when we are consistent to our convictions instead of to Christ. The error of the modern standard is that it begins at the wrong end, that is, with human reason.... We must be prepared to be led, and the way we come to an understanding is by relationship of our personal life to the Person of Jesus Christ. Then bit by bit we begin to understand.

Never have the idea that you are going to persuade men to believe in God;... Remember, along with your faithful preaching comes a thing you cannot intellectually state—the working of the Spirit of God (see John 3:8).

The thing that staggers the worker is that men will not believe. How can they believe, when our spring of life is impure? The great need is to have a channel through which the grace of God can come to men and do something in their unconscious life, then slowly as that breaks into their conscious life, there will come an expression of belief because they see Jesus.... Christian workers rarely face men in this way. You cannot argue men into coming to Jesus, or socialize them into coming. Only one thing will do it, and that is the power of the gospel drawing men by the constraint of God's grace.

The center of life and of thinking for the Christian worker is the person of Jesus Christ.... If we obey the Holy Spirit, He will bring us to face problems, and as we face them through a personal relationship to Jesus Christ, we shall go forth with courage, confident that [wherever He leads us, Jesus Christ reigns].

—*God's Workmanship*

QUESTIONS TO CONSIDER
1. What does the simplicity of the gospel mean to you?
2. How can you keep such simplicity in your spiritual walk?

A PRAYERFUL RESPONSE
Lord, help me walk and live in Your simplicity. Amen.

SHOWERS OF BLESSINGS

THOUGHT FOR TODAY

God's Word revives the dry and weary soul.

WISDOM FROM SCRIPTURE

Meanwhile his disciples urged him, "Rabbi, eat something."

But he said to them, "I have food to eat that you know nothing about."

Then his disciples said to each other, "Could someone have brought him food?"

"My food," said Jesus, "is to do the will of him who sent me and to finish his work. Do you not say, 'Four months more and then the harvest'? I tell you, open your eyes and look at the fields! They are ripe for harvest.

"Even now the reaper draws his wages, even now he harvests the crop for eternal life, so that the sower and the reaper may be glad together. Thus the saying 'One sows and another reaps' is true.

"I sent you to reap what you have not worked for. Others have done the hard work, and you have reaped the benefits of their labor."

Many of the Samaritans from that town believed in him because of the woman's testimony, "He told me everything I ever did."

So when the Samaritans came to him, they urged him to stay with them, and he stayed two days. And because of his words many more became believers.

They said to the woman, "We no longer believe just

because of what you said; now we have heard for ourselves, and we know that this man really is the Savior of the world."

JOHN 4:31-42, NIV

INSIGHTS FROM OSWALD CHAMBERS

"For as the rain cometh down and the snow from heaven, and returneth not thither, but watereth the earth, and maketh it bring forth and bud, and giveth seed to the sower and bread to the eater; so shall My word that goeth forth out of My mouth; it shall not return unto Me void, but it shall accomplish that which I please, and it shall prosper in the thing whereto I sent it" (Isaiah 55:10-11, RSV).

...God's Word is a seed. The "seed-thought" idea is one [we] need to remember. We imagine we have to plow the field, sow the seed, reap the grain, bind it into sheaves, put it through the threshing machine, make the bread—all in one discourse. "For herein is the saying true, one soweth, and another reapeth," said our Lord (John 4:37). Let each one be true to the calling given him by God.

The truth is we don't believe God can do His work without us. We are so anxious about the Word, so anxious about the people who have accepted the Word. We need not be. If we have [given] what is the Word of God, it is not our business to apply it; the Holy Spirit will apply it. Our duty is to sow the Word, see that it is the Word of God we preach, and not "huckster" it with other things. God says [His Word] will prosper in the thing whereto He sends it.

In some cases it will be a savor of life unto life, in others a savor of death unto death; but rest assured that no individual or community is the same after listening to the Word of God. It profoundly alters life. The force and power of a word of

God will work and work, and bring forth fruit after many days. Hence the necessity of revising much of what we preach and what we say in meetings.

God has not said that the relating of my experiences, of my insight into the truth, will not return to Him void. He says, "My word shall not return unto Me void." Every temptation to exalt the human, human experiences, human interests and blessings, will fall short. The only thing that prospers in God's hands is His own Word.

"As the rain cometh down from heaven, so shall My word be." Thank God for the sweet and radiant aspect of the falling rain from heaven. After a time of drought it is almost impossible to describe its beauty. So when the Word of God comes to a soul after a time of difficulty and perplexity, it is almost impossible to tell the ineffable sweetness.

—God's Workman

QUESTIONS TO CONSIDER

1. In the past, how has God planted the seed of His Word in you?
2. Do you need His showers of blessing on that seed today? If so, ask Him for it.

A PRAYERFUL RESPONSE

Lord, please plant Your Word in my heart and water it with Your blessings. Amen.

Do You Continue to Go with Jesus?

Thought for Today

We share in Christ's temptations as well as in His blessings.

Wisdom from Scripture

When the hour came, Jesus and his apostles reclined at the table.

And he said to them, "I have eagerly desired to eat this Passover with you before I suffer. For I tell you, I will not eat it again until it finds fulfillment in the kingdom of God."

After taking the cup, he gave thanks and said, "Take this and divide it among you. For I tell you I will not drink again of the fruit of the vine until the kingdom of God comes."

And he took bread, gave thanks and broke it, and gave it to them, saying, "This is my body given for you; do this in remembrance of me."

In the same way, after the supper he took the cup, saying, "This cup is the new covenant in my blood, which is poured out for you. But the hand of him who is going to betray me is with mine on the table. The Son of Man will go as it has been decreed, but woe to that man who betrays him."

They began to question among themselves which of them it might be who would do this. Also a dispute arose among them as to which of them was considered to be greatest.

Jesus said to them, "The kings of the Gentiles lord it over them; and those who exercise authority over them call themselves Benefactors. But you are not to be like that. Instead, the greatest among you should be like the youngest, and the one who rules like the one who serves.

"For who is greater, the one who is at the table or the one who serves? Is it not the one who is at the table? But I am among you as one who serves.

"You are those who have stood by me in my trials."

LUKE 22:14-28, NIV

INSIGHTS FROM OSWALD CHAMBERS

"Ye are they which have continued with me in my temptations" (Luke 22:28).

We are apt to imagine the Lord was only tempted once and then His temptations were over. His temptations went on from the first moment of His conscious life to the last because His holiness was not the holiness of Almighty God, but the holiness of men, which can only progress by the means of the things that go against it (see Hebrews 2:18; 4:15).

Are we going with Jesus in His temptations? It is true that He is with us in our temptations, but are we with Him in His?... Like Peter, we have all had moments when Jesus has had to say to us, "What, could ye not watch with me one hour?" (Matthew 26:40).

Are we lazy spiritually because we are too active in God's work? When the problems of the body face us, do we stop going with Jesus? Do we listen to the tempter's voice to put our bodily need first? It is the most subtle voice any Christian ever heard, and whether it comes through an archangel or through a man or woman, it is the voice of the devil. Are we going with Jesus along these lines, or are we putting our own needs and the needs of men and social reform first?

Satan does not come on the line of tempting us to sin, but

on the line of making us shift our point of view. Only the Spirit of God can detect this as a temptation of the devil. It is the same in missionary enterprise and in all Christian work. The Church is apt not to go with Jesus in His temptations. The temptations of our Lord in the days of His flesh are the kinds of temptations He is subjected to in the temple of our body.

Watch when God shifts your circumstances and see whether you are going with Jesus or siding with the world, the flesh, and the devil. We wear [Christ's] badge, but are we going with Him? "From that time many of his disciples went back and walked no more with Him" (John 6:66).

The temptation may be to do some "big startling thing" in order to prove that we really are the children of God. Satan said to Jesus, "If thou be the Son of God, cast thyself down from hence" (Matthew 4:6).... If by our salvation and right relationship to God, we can be the means of turning our world upside down, what has Jesus Christ been doing all these years? The temptation is to claim that God does something that will prove who we are and what He has done for us. It is a temptation of the devil, and can only be detected as a temptation by the Spirit of God.

Are we taking the pattern and print of our life from some booklet or some band of Christians, or are we continuing with Jesus, standing with Him in every new circumstance of life? It is there that we understand the fellowship of His sufferings; and the broader He makes our life and our mind and circumstances, the more essential does the one thing become— to continue with Him in His temptations.

Have we given God as much "elbow room" in our lives as our Lord gave Him in His? Have we the one set purpose which is born in us by the Son of God—not to do our own will but the will of God?... The temptations of Jesus continued all His earthly life, and they will continue all the time of His life in us....

The temptation may be to compromise with evil.... Jesus Christ was tempted like His brethren (see Hebrews 4:15), not like men who are not born again. When we are tempted as He was, do we continue to go with Him? What are we like when nobody sees? Have we a place in our heart and mind and life where there is always open communion between ourselves and God...?

Every temptation of the devil is full of the most amazing wisdom and the understanding of every problem that ever stretched before men's view. Satan's kingdom is based on wisdom; along the lines he advocates lies success, and men recognize this. Jesus Christ is not on the line of success but on the spiritual line—the holy, practical line and no other. If men and women do not continue to go with Jesus, they will begin to teach what undermines the kingdom of Jesus Christ.

...Are we compromising ... with forces that do not continue to go with Jesus, or are we maintaining the attitude of Jesus Christ all through? Are we departing from Jesus in the slightest way in connection with the world to which we belong? Have we this past week choked the Son of God in our life by imperceptible degrees? Have the demands of the life of the Son of God in us been a bit too spiritual, too strong, too sternly holy, too sternly unworldly, too pressing, too narrow, too much in the eye of God only? Or do we say, "Yes, Lord, I'll go with You all the way"?...

No matter what your circumstances may be, don't try to shield yourself from things God is bringing into your life. We have the idea sometimes that we ought to shield ourselves from some circumstances God brings around us. Never! God engineers circumstances; we have to see that we face them abiding continually with Him in His temptations. They are His temptations; they are not temptations to us, but to the Son of God in us.... Are we going with Jesus in His temptations in our bodies? Are we going with Him in the temptations of our mental and moral life, and of our spiritual life, abiding true to God all through? This is the one concern Jesus Christ has about us....

Do you continue to go with Jesus? The way lies through Gethsemane, through the city gate, outside the camp. The way lies alone, and the way lies until there is no trace of a footstep left, only the voice saying, "Follow Me."

—The Love of God

Questions to Consider
1. How is Christ asking you to share in His temptations?
2. Will you continue to go with Jesus? Why, or why not?

A Prayerful Response
Lord, I will share in Your temptations and continue witn You. Amen.

BOOKS BY OSWALD CHAMBERS

Approved Unto God
Baffled to Fight Better
Biblical Ethics
Biblical Psychology
Bringing Sons Into Glory
Christian Disciplines
Conformed to His Image
Disciples Indeed
Facing Reality
God's Workmanship
If Thou Wilt Be Perfect
If Ye Shall Ask
Knocking at God's Door
Making All Things New
My Utmost for His Highest
Not Knowing Whither
Our Brilliant Heritage
Run Today's Race
Shade of His Hand
So Send I You
Studies in the Sermon on the Mount
The Highest Good
The Love of God
Moral Foundations of Life
The Philosophy of Sin
The Place of Help
The Psychology of Redemption
The Servant and His Lord
The Shadow of an Agony
Workmen of God

ABOUT THE COMPILER

With the *Life Messages of Great Christians* series, Judith Couchman hopes you'll be encouraged and enlightened by people who have shared their spiritual journeys through the printed word.

Judith owns Judith & Company, an editorial consulting and writing business. Prior to this, she was the creator and founding editor-in-chief of *Clarity* magazine, managing editor of *Christian Life*, editor of *Sunday Digest*, director of communications for The Navigators, and director of new product development for the periodicals group of NavPress.

Besides speaking to women's and professional conferences, Judith has written or compiled fourteen books and many magazine articles. In addition, she has received numerous awards for her work in secondary education, religious publishing, and corporate communications.

She lives in Colorado.